Integrating Science & Literature

by Judith Cochran

Incentive Publications
Nashville, Tennessee

Cover and illustrations by Cheryl Mendenhall
Edited by Jan Keeling

ISBN 0-86530-198-0

TABLE OF CONTENTS

Preface

This book offers a new way to integrate literature into the standard curriculum: using literature selections as springboards for scientific exploration and discovery. Every selection is presented in a carefully-organized, easy-to-understand format. Each book treatment was designed to reinforce a scientific concept, and contains these components:

Teacher's Guide
The Teacher's Guide page consists of a brief summary of the book, suggestions for pre- and postreading discussions, and a simple science experiment or concept presentation.

Science Activities
The Science Activities page is filled with activities geared to individual student work, or for students working in pairs, in cooperative groups, or as a whole group.

Student Pages
Each selection is complete with one or two reproducible pages intended for use by the student. The use of these pages will apply and reinforce the scientific concept under discussion.

Thematic Activities
A page of thematic activities broadens the scope of the book by outlining simple, enjoyable activities related to other subject areas: Writing, Language Arts, Mathematics, Social Studies, and Fine Arts.

Each activity is keyed to Bloom's Taxonomy of higher level thinking and is marked with an abbreviation denoting the specific level it reinforces:

K = Knowledge	**An** = Analysis
C = Comprehension	**Sy** = Synthesis
Ap = Application	**Ev** = Evaluation

As you use this unique science resource in your classroom, you will see your students learn and enjoy as the reading of a story leads to brainstorming and discussion, measuring, weighing, observing, and creating.

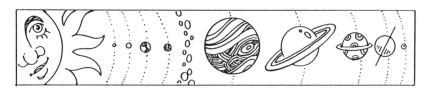

INCH BY INCH

Summary: An inchworm proves useful for measuring things. He even measures his way out of danger.

PREREADING DISCUSSION:

How long do you think an inchworm is? How long do you think an inch is? How long do you think 5 inches is? (Have children approximate the lengths on their own.) This is the story of an inchworm who measures many things. See how long the inchworm is. How long are the things that he measures?

POSTREADING DISCUSSION:

How long do you think an inch is now? How long is five inches? What other things can be measured in inches? (Discuss.)

 EXPERIMENT:
Candy Worm Measurement

You will need:
- 1 candy worm (jelly candy shaped like a worm) per child
- Pencils
- Crayons
- Student reproducible page 11

An **Additional Activity**

Discuss other things that can or cannot be measured with candy worms. Explain why.

You will be asked to:

1. Draw your candy worms actual size. (Encourage the children to be very observant about color, shape, and length.)

2. Use your candy worms to measure these things:
   - your arms (length or circumference)
   - desk (width, length or height)
   - chair
   - shoe
   - pencil
   - paper, etc.

3. Record and graph results on student reproducible page 11.

Can	Can't / Why
trees	amount of water—not length
sidewalk	gallons of gas—not length
window	miles a car goes—too far / worm too short

INCH BY INCH

MEASURE THIS, MEASURE THAT – PAIRS OR COOPERATIVE GROUPS

C/Ap

You will be given lengths of yarn one inch, one foot, and one foot, and one yard long. Go out around school to measure and record different things, such as hopscotch pattern, four-square courts, or sandboxes. Discuss and record the measurements on charts in class.

HOW TALL ARE YOU? – INDIVIDUALS OR PAIRS

C/Ap

Have someone outline your body on a length of butcher paper. Then measure your overall length (as drawn on the butcher paper) with rulers or yardsticks, then your arms, legs, feet, hands, head, recording the lengths as you measure.

GRAPHING – PAIRS, COOPERATIVE GROUPS, OR WHOLE GROUP

Ap/An

Graph the results of various measuring experiences.

How Tall Are You?

39 in. ■■■□□□□□□□□□
42 in. ■■■■■■■■■■■□
45 in. ■■■■■■■□□□□□
etc.

1 2 3 4 5 6 7 8 9 10 11 12
Number of Students

How Long?

	inches	feet	yards
hopscotch	36	3	1
foursquare	60	5	1²/₃
sandbox	144	12	4

(Ask questions: "Who is tallest?" "How many people are 39 inches tall?" "Which is longer, hopscotch or four-square?", etc.)

ESTIMATION – INDIVIDUALS, PAIRS, OR COOPERATIVE GROUPS

Ap/An

(Give children experiences with estimated length.)
Examples:
"Draw a red box three inches long."
"Make a house five inches high."
"Lift your leg one foot off the ground."
"Hold your hand two feet from your face."

(Measure the exact distance/length only after you've estimated it. This is a fun "filler" activity, and should be used often so students can internalize and understand measurement.)

INCH BY INCH

Draw your candy worm actual size.

Measure these things:

arm _____
desk _____
chair _____
door _____

shoe _____
pencil _____
paper _____
book _____

Graph the results:

arm

desk

chair

door

shoe

pencil

paper

book

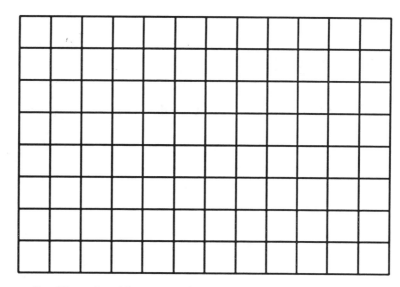

2 2½ 3 3½ 4 4½ 5 5½ 6 6½ 7 7½

Measurement in candy worms

Which is the longest? _____

Which is the shortest? _____

Name _____

INCH BY INCH

Cut out the ruler below. Use it to find the following things:

1. Something that measures 3 inches.

   This _____ is 3 inches.

2. Something that measures 6 inches.

   This _____ is 6 inches.

3. Something that measures 8 inches.

   This _____ is 8 inches.

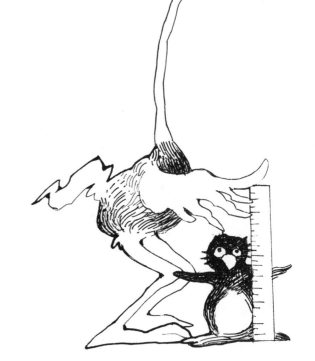

4. Draw these things:

   A cat 2 inches long   A snake 1½ inches long   A cup 1 inch tall

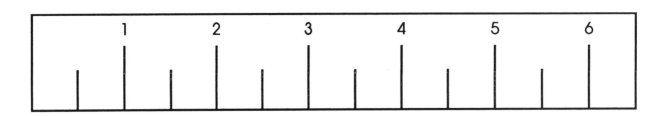

Name _____

INCH BY INCH

WRITING

Ap **Group Activity:** If you were the inchworm, what kinds of things would you measure? (List on board. Model writing sentences from student responses.)

Ap **Pre-Writers:** Draw some of the things you would measure if you were an inchworm. Copy and complete this sentence:
"I would measure _____ and _____ ."

Ap **Beginning Writers:** Draw and list three things you would measure if you were an inchworm.

Ap **Experienced Writers:** Write about five things you would measure if you were an inchworm. Draw them.

LANGUAGE ARTS

Sy **Candy Worm Stories:** Make up a story in which your candy worm measures things.

Ev **What Happened Next?** Write story chains about what might have happened to the inchworm after the end of *Inch By Inch*.

MATHEMATICS

Ap/An **Cut, Count, and Compare Feet:** Trace around one of your feet and cut out the shape. Use it to measure different things, then compare your "foot" measure to a standard foot measure. (Discuss how standard measurement solves many problems.)

SOCIAL STUDIES

C **Cubits and Things:** Study units of measurement that have been used throughout history. (Example: A cubit was the length between a person's elbow and the tips of his or her fingers.)

FINE ARTS

Ap **Clay Creations:** Make clay creations to certain specified heights, lengths, widths (example: a fish 2 inches long).

HOW MUCH IS A MILLION?

Summary: The reader of this book will gain perspective on the numbers one million, a billion, and a trillion.

PREREADING DISCUSSION:

How high can you count? How long do you think it would take you to count to 100? 1000? 1,000,000? (Discuss.) This book gives us some idea of how much a million, billion, and a trillion are. Listen to how big these numbers are.

POSTREADING DISCUSSION:

How big does a fishbowl have to be to hold a million fish? (Discuss.)

 CONCEPT:
How Many?

You will need:
- Pencil for each child
- Calculators (if possible)
- Student reproducible page 16

1. Working as a class, count together as far as you can in 5 minutes. Write down the final number. Then calculate how long it would take to count to 1,000; 100,000; and 1,000,000.

2. Calculate how many days you have lived. (Show the children how to calculate an approximate number, based on 365 days in a year. Use addition if multiplication isn't known.)

EXAMPLE:

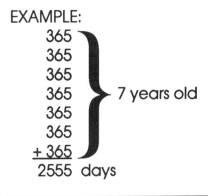

$$
\left.\begin{array}{r}
365 \\
365 \\
365 \\
365 \\
365 \\
365 \\
+\,365 \\
\hline
2555
\end{array}\right\} 7 \text{ years old}
$$

2555 days

3. The teacher will select a child and count how many times his or her heart beats in a minute. As a class, calculate how many times the heart would beat in an hour, a day, a year, a whole life.

HOW MUCH IS A MILLION?

BEAN STICKS – PAIRS, COOPERATIVE GROUPS, WHOLE GROUPS

`Ap`

You will need: box of popsicle sticks, glue, beans. Glue ten beans on each stick. Once they are dry, you can manipulate them into groups of 100; 500; 1,000; etc. See how high you can go!

PENNY WISE – PAIRS OR COOPERATIVE GROUPS

`C/Ap`

Start a class "penny drive," by either collecting pennies or selling things for pennies. Use paper bank rolls to count out 100 pennies and package them. See how much money you have and how many pennies it took to arrive at this amount.

SEE STARS – PAIRS, COOPERATIVE GROUPS, OR WHOLE GROUP

`C`

Each child will fold a piece of paper into eight sections. Draw ten stars on each section and cut the sections out. Paste them together in groups of 100, then arrange them on a bulletin board into groups of 1,000. See how many stars it takes to cover the whole bulletin board.

ESTIMATING AND GRAPHING – PAIRS OR COOPERATIVE GROUPS

`An`

Each pair or group will receive a watermelon or a pumpkin. Once the melon is open, estimate the number of seeds inside and record your estimation. Working together, count the seeds, placing them in groups of ten. After noting your results, record them on a class graph. As a final activity, calculate how many seeds there are altogether.

HOW MANY? THIS MANY! – COOPERATIVE GROUPS OR WHOLE GROUP

`C/Ap`

Everyone will bring in different-sized containers and bags of beans. Count the beans into containers, making sure they are in groups of 100 (this makes calculating easier). See how many hundreds of beans fill each container, and add up the numbers to see how many there are altogether.

<u>Extra Challenge</u>: Start a collection of containers with 1000 beans in each one. See how close to 100,000 or 1,000,000 beans you can get.

THOUSAND BEAN CHILI – COOPERATIVE GROUPS OR WHOLE GROUP

`Ap`

Cook up a batch of chili, using 1000 or 10,000 beans. See how much chili this makes and how many it serves. Then calculate how many beans are in each serving. This can be a great fund-raiser or culminating activity for your *How Much Is A Million?* unit.

HOW MUCH IS A MILLION?

Ap

1. How high can you count in 5 minutes? _____

   How long would it take to count to: 1,000? _____

   Do your math here: 100,000? _____

                                           1,000,000? _____

2. There are 365 days in a year. How many days have you lived? _____

   Do your math here:

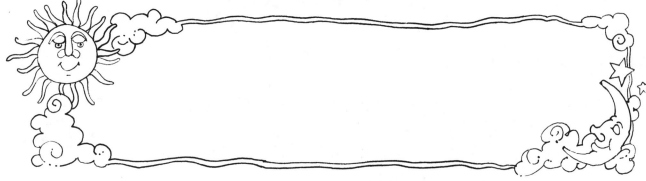

3. How many times does your heart beat in: Do your math here:

   a minute? _____

   an hour? _____

   a day? _____

   a year? _____

   How many times has it beat in your life? _____

Name _____

HOW MUCH IS A MILLION?

Color these fish. Add more to make 100.

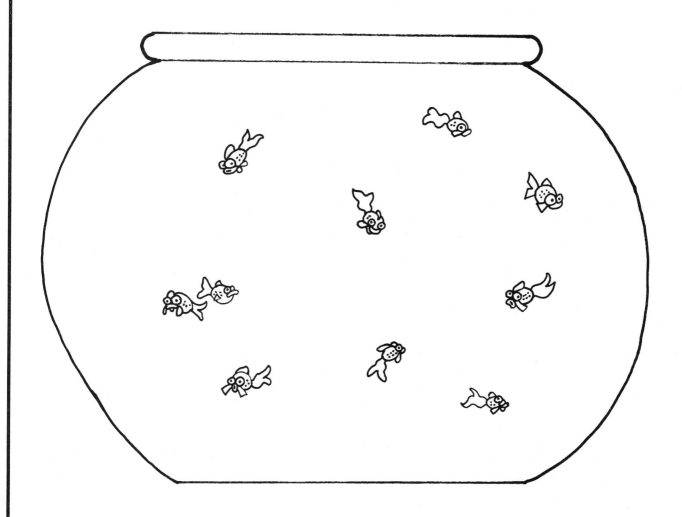

How many fish do 5 kids have? _____

How many fish do 10 kids have? _____

How many fish does your whole class have? _____

HOW MUCH IS A MILLION?

WRITING

Ap **Group Activity:** How high can you write your numbers? (Model writing sequential numbers for the level of your students, e.g., 1, 2, 3, or 101, 102, 103, or 1001, 1002, 1003. NOTE: Older children respond well to a timed challenge such as, "How far can you write in 5 minutes?")

Ap **Pre-Writers:** Write your numbers as high as you can.

Ap **Beginning Writers:** Write your numbers as high as you can.

Ap **Experienced Writers:** Write your numbers as high as you can.

LANGUAGE ARTS

Sy **Counting Rhymes:** Make up rhymes for numbers considerably higher than the ones in "1, 2, buckle my shoe." (Example: "1000, 1001, I stepped on my thumb.")

C/Ap **Read About It:** Read books that can be related to numbers or things you can count. (Examples: "Count how many animals there are in *Animals Born Alive And Well*," or "How many clouds are in *The Cloud Book*?"

MATHEMATICS

C/Ap **Place Value:** Learn place values up to one million (1,000,000). Solve simple addition and subtraction problems that have many zeros.

Examples:

$$\begin{array}{r} 100{,}000 \\ +\underline{840{,}000} \end{array} \quad \text{or} \quad \begin{array}{r} 1{,}000{,}000 \\ +\underline{1{,}000{,}000} \end{array}$$

Ap **Add 'Em Up:** Work some of the calculations given in a math book.

C **Collection:** The class will collect small items such as bottle caps or corks. Your goal may be 10,000; 100,000; or 1,000,000.

SOCIAL STUDIES

Ap **Mapping Miles:** Calculate the distance from New York to New Zealand, and the distances between other cities around the globe.

FINE ARTS

Ap **Stick Towers:** Build towers, each made of 100 popsicle sticks or toothpicks. Once finished, place towers on top of one another in order to gain perspective on the numbers of sticks used.

GREGORY, THE TERRIBLE EATER

Summary: Gregory the goat doesn't want to eat the tin cans and trash his parents offer; instead he would rather eat food such as carrots and oranges. Together, he and his parents solve his problem.

PREREADING DISCUSSION:

K/Ev

What kinds of foods would you eat if you were a terrible eater? What kinds of foods do you think a goat would eat if he were a terrible eater? (Discuss.) This is the story of Gregory, a goat who is a terrible eater. Listen carefully to the story of the "terrible" food he eats.

POSTREADING DISCUSSION:

C/An

What were some of the "terrible" foods that Gregory ate? (List on board.)

K CONCEPT:
The Four Food Groups

The four food groups consist of:
1. Meat and Beans
2. Breads and Cereals
3. Fruit and Vegetables
4. Milk

1. The MEAT & BEANS group contains:
steak
chicken
peanut butter
ham
fish
nuts
hot dogs
hamburger patties
lunchmeat
eggs
tofu
beans

2. The BREADS & CEREALS group contains:
bread
rice
grits
oatmeal
tortillas
biscuits
potatoes
bagels
hot dog buns
muffins
crackers
popcorn
graham crackers
breakfast cereal
hamburger buns

3. The FRUITS & VEGETABLES group contains:
all fruits and vegetables, including juices and dried fruit/vegetables

4. The MILK group contains:

cheese	buttermilk	yogurt	cottage cheese
pudding	ice cream	milk	

GREGORY, THE TERRIBLE EATER

WEEK-AT-A-GLANCE – INDIVIDUALS OR PAIRS

Chart what you've had for breakfast, lunch, and dinner each day for a week. (Younger children may chart what they had for one meal each day. Breakfast or lunch is easiest for them to remember.)

CATEGORIZING – PAIRS, COOPERATIVE GROUPS

An

Draw on cards the food and things Gregory ate. Categorize them as many different ways as possible, recording your work.

TASTING PARTY – WHOLE GROUP

C/Sy

Taste the different foods from each food group that the teacher will bring to class. Record your impressions of each food (its texture, color, smell, taste, etc.).

MEAL-FOR-A-DAY – COOPERATIVE GROUPS OR WHOLE GROUP

Ap

Working together, design a series of well-balanced meals that could be served in the cafeteria. Contact the person in charge of cafeteria meals and see if it would be possible to serve one of the meals designed by your class. (You might be surprised to know how many cafeteria supervisors are happy to go along with activities like this one.)

CUT-AND-PASTE – INDIVIDUALS OR PAIRS

Divide a piece of paper into 4 sections, labeling each section as one of the food groups. Cut pictures of food from magazines and paste them into the proper sections.

GREGORY, THE TERRIBLE EATER

Draw foods for each food group.

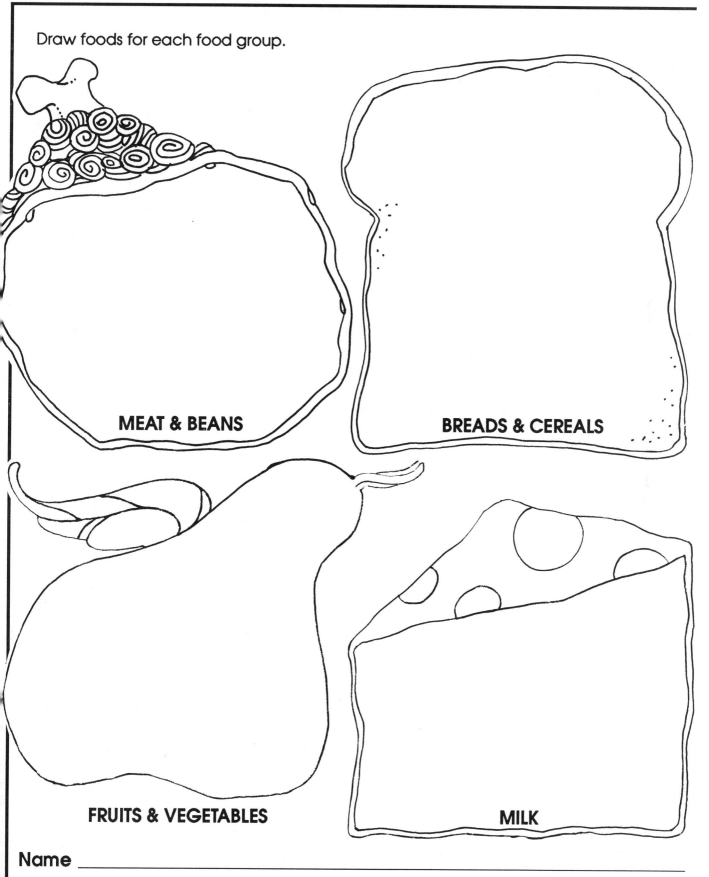

MEAT & BEANS

BREADS & CEREALS

FRUITS & VEGETABLES

MILK

Name _____

GREGORY, THE TERRIBLE EATER

WRITING

Ev **Group Activity – What If?** If you were Gregory, what are some <u>foods</u> you would want to eat? What are some <u>things</u> you would want to eat? (Draw or list these things on the board. Model writing sentences from the ideas generated.)

Ev **Pre-Writers:** Draw what you would eat if you were Gregory. Make sure you include both <u>food</u> and <u>things</u>. Copy and complete this sentence:

"I want to eat _____ and _____ ."

Ev **Beginning Writers:** Draw and list the elements of a meal of <u>food</u> and <u>things</u> you would eat if you were Gregory.

Ev **Experienced Writers:** Write about all the <u>food</u> and <u>things</u> you would eat if you were Gregory. Illustrate your story.

LANGUAGE ARTS

Ap **Paired Reading:** Working in pairs, take turns reading *Gregory, The Terrible Eater* to each other.

Sy **Puppet Show:** Working with a small group, put on a puppet show retelling the story of Gregory and the different foods he ate.

MATHEMATICS

An **Graphing:** Determine the food groups from which each child selected his or her breakfast foods, and make a class graph of this information.

SOCIAL STUDIES

An **Similarities/Differences:** Discuss the different types of foods the class members eat at home and which nationalities may be represented. Show the similarities among all the different types of foods by grouping them into the four food groups.

FINE ARTS

C/Ap **Picture This Meal:** Cut out food pictures from magazines and paste them on paper plates to show balanced meals.

BREAD AND JAM FOR FRANCES

Summary: Frances wants nothing but bread and jam to eat all day long. Mother comes up with a good plan to get Frances to eat good food again.

PREREADING DISCUSSION:

Ap

Do you know someone who's a picky eater? Do you know someone who only wants to eat junk food? (Discuss.) This is about Frances, who is a picky eater. Listen to the story about the food she eats and what happens to her.

POSTREADING DISCUSSION:

C/Ev

What did Frances eat that could be called "junk food"? (List on board.) What happened to her? (Discuss.) What are some other junk foods? (List on board.) What do you think might happen if you ate only junk food? (Discuss.)

C/Ap **EXPERIMENT:**
What Is Junk Food?

READ THE INGREDIENTS

You will need:
- Cereal boxes
- Candy wrappers (gather wrappers from playground)
- Other food cartons
- Student reproducible page 25

Other names for sugar are:
- sugar
- corn syrup
- corn sweetener
- dextrose
- sucrose
- fructose
- honey

Other names for fat are:
- vegetable oil
- hydrogenated oil
- peanut oil
- soybean oil
- coconut oil
- lard
- palm oil

Junk food is food that contains too much sugar or fat. To find out if a food is healthful or not, you need to read the ingredients on the label. If one of the first three (3) ingredients listed is sugar or fat, the food is "junk."

BREAD AND JAM FOR FRANCES

GOOD FOOD PRODUCT – INDIVIDUALS, PAIRS, OR COOPERATIVE GROUPS

`Ap/Ev`

Make up your own good food product, design a package for it, and list its ingredients on the package. Share your ideas with the class.

RADIO/TELEVISION SURVEY – INDIVIDUALS OR PAIRS

`An`

Keep a tally of the kinds of foods that are advertised on radio and television. Add individual tallies together to form a class tally, and draw conclusions about what America is being asked to buy. Discuss the tactics the ads use ("You're smart if you buy," "You'll have more energy," "Make more friends," "It simply tastes good"…).

LUNCHTIME = JUNK FOOD OR GOOD FOOD? – PAIRS, COOPERATIVE GROUPS, OR WHOLE GROUP

`Ap/Ev`

Gather wrappers from a day's trash around the lunchroom and schoolyard. Read the ingredients on the wrappers and categorize the foods they once contained into "good food" or "junk food." Use this information to determine the kinds of foods most people are eating at school.

IT PAYS TO ADVERTISE – PAIRS OR COOPERATIVE GROUPS

`Sy`

Make up posters and write radio advertisements for good food habits (eating fruits, vegetables, a balanced diet, etc.). Place the posters around the school and community. Tape record the radio ads. Contact local stations to see if they will air some of these ads.

YOU ARE WHAT YOU EAT – PAIRS, COOPERATIVE GROUPS, OR WHOLE GROUP

`Sy`

Generate ideas about what can happen if you eat a diet of junk food instead of a diet of good food.

BREAD AND JAM FOR FRANCES

Draw a food item wrapper in each box and list below the box the first three ingredients in each item. Circle JF for junk food and GF for good food.

JF or GF

Ingredients:

1. _____
2. _____
3. _____

JF or GF

Ingredients:

1. _____
2. _____
3. _____

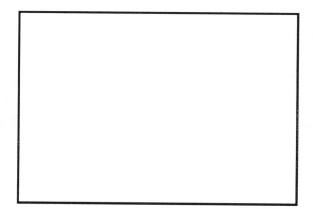

JF or GF

Ingredients:

1. _____
2. _____
3. _____

JF or GF

Ingredients:

1. _____
2. _____
3. _____

Name _____

BREAD AND JAM FOR FRANCES

WRITING

Sy **Group Activity – Letter Writing:** Write a group letter to Frances about her eating habits.

Sy **Pre-Writers:** Draw a picture of junk food. Copy and complete this letter form:
"Dear Frances,
I am glad you don't eat _____."

Sy **Beginning Writers:** Draw a picture for and write a letter to Frances.

Sy **Experienced Writers:** Write a letter to Frances about what she eats. Illustrate it when you're finished.

LANGUAGE ARTS

C/Sy **Jumprope Rhymes:** Practice some of the rhymes Frances sings in the story. (Encourage children to make up their own rhymes.)

Sy **Commercial:** Write commercials for healthful food and act them out.

MATHEMATICS

Ap **Measuring:** Follow recipes to prepare healthful snacks, measuring out the ingredients.

SOCIAL STUDIES

An **Similarities/Differences:** Discuss how mealtimes at Frances's house are both similar to and different from mealtimes at children's homes.

FINE ARTS

Sy **Junk Food Sculpture:** Put together a sculpture or bulletin board, using junk food wrappers and trash found around school.

Sy **Posters:** Design posters advertising healthful foods and snacks. Place them around the school and community.

MUNCHING, POEMS ABOUT EATING

Summary: *Spaghetti, bananas and cream, drinking a salad . . .* Poems about eating and food will delight those who enjoy a good rhyme.

PREREADING DISCUSSION:

What are some of your favorite foods that are both good for you and fun to munch? (Discuss.) This book contains many poems about eating. Listen to the story and see if any of your favorite foods or snacks are mentioned.

POSTREADING DISCUSSION:

C

What were some of the foods mentioned in the poems? (Write on board. Examples: spaghetti, pizza, bananas and cream, milk, carrots, eggs, hot dogs.)

 EXPERIMENT:
Healthful Snack-Tasting Experience

You will need:
- Popcorn
- Cheese cubes
- Carrot sticks
- Crackers
- Fruit juice
- Fruit leather
- Paper plates and cups
- Student reproducible page 29

1. Put a little of everything on your plate.

2. Taste everything and record your results on the reproducible page 29.

3. Contribute to a class graph of the taste test results.

FAVORITE SNACKS

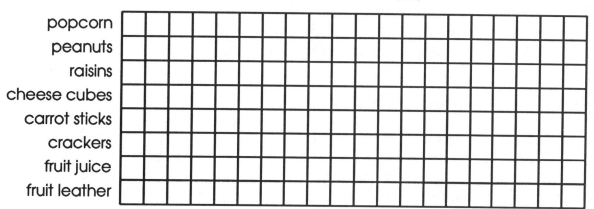

MUNCHING, POEMS ABOUT EATING

MAKE IT AND SELL IT – COOPERATIVE GROUPS OR WHOLE GROUP

`C/Ap`
Make popular healthful snacks and sell them during lunchtime. Use this activity as a fundraiser to raise money for a field trip that has something to do with healthful eating.

SALAD DAYS – INDIVIDUALS OR PAIRS

`Ap`
Read the poem "Drink a Garden." The teacher will provide a number of different salad items such as lettuce, carrots, mushrooms, beets, onions, sunflower seeds, raisins, and cabbage. (Set them up like a salad bar and let students make their own salads.)

GROW IT AND EAT IT – COOPERATIVE GROUPS OR WHOLE GROUP

`Ap`
Plant seeds used to grow favorite foods (such as carrots, watermelons, corn, beans, lettuce). Take care of them and watch them grow. Learn more about plants (see section on plants, pages 60-73). Harvest your "crops" and eat them.

TRAIL MIX – INDIVIDUALS OR PAIRS

`K`
The teacher will provide ingredients for making trail mix (raisins, nuts, seeds, and dried fruit). Mix your own trail mix in a small cup, recording what you put into it.

RECIPE BOOK – COOPERATIVE GROUPS OR WHOLE GROUP

`Ap/Sy`
The teacher will compile recipes for healthful snacks that children can safely make. (Don't include anything that requires cooking except for foods that may be put in a toaster.) Working with your group, write up the recipes, illustrate them, and compile them into a healthful snack recipe book.

MUNCHING, POEMS ABOUT EATING   An/Ev

Draw and write the names of the snacks you tasted.
Circle the face that shows how you liked each one.

The snacks I liked best were _____

_____

Name _____

MUNCHING, POEMS ABOUT EATING `K/C`

HEALTHFUL SNACKS

Here are some snacks that are good for you and that taste good too!

Banana Smoothie

- 1 cup milk
- 1 banana
- 1 Tbsp. honey or sugar

1. Put all ingredients in a blender. Blend well.
2. Drink and enjoy.

Note: You can make this drink with other fruits too.

Peanut Butter/ Honey Toast

- 1 slice bread
- raisins
- 1 Tbsp. peanut butter
- 1 tsp. honey

1. Toast bread in toaster.
2. Mix together peanut butter and honey.
3. Spread mixture on toast. Dot with raisins.

Popsicles

- 1 lg. can frozen orange juice
- 1½ juice cans water
- 1 carton flavored yogurt

1. Mix everything and pour into paper cups.
2. Add a stick and freeze.

Other Great Snacks

- popcorn
- yogurt
- crackers
- raisins
- fruit
- grapes
- apples
- fruit cocktail
- fruit juices
- nuts
- sunflower seeds
- carrot sticks
- vegetables
- pudding
- cheese

MUNCHING, POEMS ABOUT EATING

WRITING

Sy

Group Activity: Working as a group, write a cinquain about one of the foods mentioned in the book.

EXAMPLE: Spaghetti (one-word title)
Long noodles (two words defining title)
Wavy, slurpy, tomato-y (three descriptive words)
Ummy, yummy (two words expressing feeling)
Spaghetti (repeat title)

Ap/Sy

Pre-Writers: Draw a favorite food and dictate a cinquain about it OR copy the group cinquain and draw a picture for it.

Sy

Beginning Writers: Draw your favorite food and write a cinquain about it.

Sy

Experienced Writers: Write a cinquain about your favorite food. Illustrate your work.

LANGUAGE ARTS

Ap

Recipes: Bring in recipes for healthful snacks.

Ap

Class Cookbook: Compile class recipes into a class cookbook.

An

Tell How: Cook together in small groups. One child in the group will explain how to prepare a healthful snack and the others will follow his or her directions.

MATHEMATICS

C

Add/Subtract: After reading the poem "At The Table," work some addition/subtraction problems using healthful snacks such as raisins, nuts, and popcorn as manipulatives.

Ap

Measuring: Learn how to measure in cups, tablespoons, and teaspoons.

SOCIAL STUDIES

K

Chopsticks: After reading the poem "Eats," practice eating food with chopsticks. Learn about the cultures whose people use chopsticks and about the foods these people eat with the chopsticks.

FINE ARTS

Sy

Popcorn Art: Draw or paint an outdoor scene of trees and clouds, etc. Decorate your scene with popcorn, pasting it onto the clouds, using it for flowers, and for buds on trees.

Sy

Posters: Make posters showing healthful snacks. Put them up around school.

SUMMER IS . . .

Summary: These are heartwarming poems about the sights and pleasures of each season.

PREREADING DISCUSSION:

Ap

What is your favorite season? Why? What kinds of colors, sounds, and feelings does the thought of each season bring to mind? (Discuss.) This is a book by a woman who thinks of many things that are related to each season. Listen to the way she writes of the colors, tastes, and smells the seasons have for her.

POSTREADING DISCUSSION:

Ap

What are some of the colors, tastes, smells, and feeling of each season? (Discuss. Write them on the board.)

K/C **EXPERIMENT:**
Seasons Caused By Tilt Of Earth

You will need:
- A flashlight
- A globe
- Chalk
- Blackboard
- Student reproducible page 34

1. Shine the flashlight on the globe, tilting North America toward the flashlight. The light will be more concentrated on that area: It is summer in North America.

2. Keep the flashlight shining on the globe and tilt North America away from the light. The light will now be more diffused: It is winter in North America. When the tilt of the earth is between these two extremes, it means it is autumn or spring.

3. Shine the flashlight directly on the chalkboard. Trace around the edges of the light—this is *concentrated* light, making it hot (summer). Now shine the flashlight at an angle and trace around it on the blackboard. This light is *diffused*, making it cooler (winter).

SUMMER IS . . .

MAGAZINE DETECTIVE – PAIRS OR COOPERATIVE GROUPS

An

Cut out magazine pictures that clearly show the seasons. Cluster the pictures on a bulletin board to form a class collage, making four groups of pictures to show the four seasons.

WEATHER WATCHER – INDIVIDUALS, PAIRS, COOPERATIVE GROUPS, OR WHOLE GROUP

Ap/An

Discuss the different types of weather to be found in each season. Then record the weather daily for a week. Discuss how it varies, even if it fits the typical weather for its season. (For more detailed information, see the section on WEATHER, p. 42)

MOVED BY THE EARTH AND SUN – COOPERATIVE GROUPS OR WHOLE GROUP

K

Learn about the movements the earth makes. (It rotates once every 24 hours to form day and night; it revolves about the sun once a year, resulting in the seasons. For more detailed information, see the section on the SOLAR SYSTEM, pp. 135-138.)

SIGNS OF THE SEASON – COOPERATIVE GROUPS OR WHOLE GROUP

Ap/An

Discuss the characteristics of the season you are now experiencing (flowers that may be blooming, what the trees look like, which animals are flourishing). Write these characteristics on the board. Then take a walk around the schoolyard and neighborhood, looking for all the signs of the season. When you return to the classroom, circle all the things you observed and add new characteristics to your list.

DAYS LONGER, DAYS SHORTER – WHOLE GROUP

K

Discuss what happens to the length of the day during different seasons (days are longer in summer, and shorter in winter).

Winter Solstice: shortest day of the year   **Spring Equinox:** day and night are of equal length
Summer Solstice: longest day of the year   **Fall Equinox:** day and night are of equal length

ANIMALS HIBERNATE – COOPERATIVE GROUPS OR WHOLE GROUP

K/Ap

Learn about the animals who hibernate during the short days of winter. Act out what these animals do so that they won't starve during their long sleep. You may also: • Make dioramas of their homes.
⠀⠀⠀⠀⠀⠀⠀⠀• Bring samples of their food.
⠀⠀⠀⠀⠀⠀⠀⠀• Tell about a day in the life of such an animal in the summer, and about a day in winter.

SUMMER IS . . .

Draw the way the light is shining on the tilted globes below.

It is _____ in North America.

It is _____ in North America.

Draw each kind of light.

Concentrated Light

Diffused Light

Concentrated light from the sun causes which season?_____

Diffused light from the sun causes which season?_____

Name _____

SUMMER IS . . .

Draw and write about each season.

In Summer _____

_____

In Autumn _____

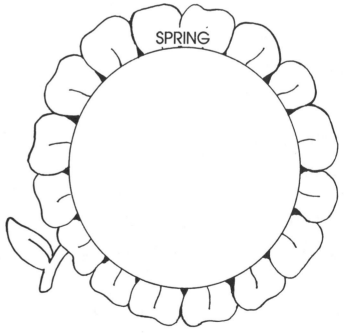

In Winter _____

_____

In Spring _____

_____

Name _____

SUMMER IS . . .

WRITING

Sy **Group Activity:** Using the lists generated in the postreading discussion, think of sentences that describe colors, tastes, smells, sounds, and/or sights of a season. (Model writing these ideas in sentences. Examples: Fall is orange. It tastes like apples and smells like popcorn.)

Sy **Pre-Writers:** Draw a favorite thing about your favorite season. Copy and complete the following sentences:

"_____ (season) is _____ (color).

It tastes (or sounds or looks) like _____."

Sy **Beginning Writers:** Draw pictures of and write about your favorite season.

Sy **Experienced Writers:** Write about the color, taste, smell, sound, sight, and feeling of your favorite season. Illustrate your work.

LANGUAGE ARTS

Sy **Give A Riddle / Make A Rhyme:** Make up a riddle or rhyme about each season without mentioning the season's name. Ask others to guess the seasons that inspired your riddles and rhymes.

MATHEMATICS

An/Ev **Autumn Leaves:** The teacher will bring in to school many autumn leaves of different shapes and colors. Estimate the number of leaves of each kind. Check out your estimate.

SOCIAL STUDIES

C/An **Adaptation:** Discuss how people adapt to each season by changing the things they do, the food they eat, and the clothes they wear.

FINE ARTS

Ap/Sy **A Tree All Year:** Draw a tree four times, showing how it appears each season.

THOMAS' SNOWSUIT

Summary: Thomas' mother has bought him a snowsuit he doesn't want to wear. Getting him into the snowsuit turns into a wrestling match. A funny story!

PREREADING DISCUSSION:

What kinds of clothes do you wear in the summer, fall, winter, spring? (Discuss.) This is a story about Thomas and the snowsuit his mother bought him. Watch for the different kinds of clothes worn by the people in the story.

POSTREADING DISCUSSION:

What kinds of clothes were worn by the people in the story? (List on board.)

 CONCEPT:
Dress According To The Weather

Your choice of what to wear may depend on what the weather is like outside. You would not wear a bathing suit when it is snowing.

When it's hot, it is best to wear things that keep you cool:

sandals   hat   tee-shirt   sunglasses   shorts

When it rains, you wear things to keep you dry:

umbrella   boots   rain hat   raincoat   pants

When it snows, you ought to wear things that keep you warm:

sweater   scarf   snowsuit   hat   gloves

THOMAS' SNOWSUIT

WEATHER PERSON – WHOLE GROUP

C/Ap

The teacher will provide an outline of a person and cutouts of different types of clothes. Along with morning calendar activities, "clothe" the person in clothes that are appropriate for the weather.

DRESS UP – PAIRS, COOPERATIVE GROUPS, OR WHOLE GROUP

Ap

The teacher will provide a wide variety of seasonal dress-up clothes. Dress up, explain what you are wearing, and tell what the weather would be like for you to dress the way you are.

WEARING BEARLY ANYTHING – INDIVIDUALS, PAIRS, OR COOPERATIVE GROUPS

An

Bring to school stuffed animals or dolls dressed for different types of weather. Discuss the clothing and determine the weather each type is suited for. Classify the toys according to clothing and weather type.

GRAPH IT – COOPERATIVE GROUPS OR WHOLE GROUP

An

Make a graph of the weather preferences of all the children in the class, then make a graph of everyone's favorite clothes. Compare the data to see if the favorite clothing chart correlates to the favorite weather chart.

FAVORITE WEATHER

sunny							
rainy							
cold							
windy							
snowing							

FAVORITE CLOTHES

shorts							
t-shirt							
boots							
coats							
sandals							

DARK COLORS / LIGHT COLORS – COOPERATIVE GROUPS OR WHOLE GROUP

K/C

Discuss how dark colors absorb light to keep you warm, and how light colors reflect light to keep you cool. (That is why people wear dark colors in the winter and lighter colors in the summer.)

Experiment
You will need:

2 paper cups   Black paper
Tape   White paper
Ice cubes   Scissors

1. Put black paper around one cup. Wrap white paper around the other.
2. Fill each with ice cubes. Set in sun.
3. Check after 15 minutes and 30 minutes. Which cup's ice has melted the most? Why?

COTTON AND WOOL – PAIRS, COOPERATIVE GROUPS, OR WHOLE GROUP

K

Cotton comes from a plant. It is light, and good for spring / summer wear. Wool comes from sheep. It is heavier, and is good for keeping people warm, even when the weather is wet. Check the labels on your summer and winter clothing to see what they are made of.

THOMAS' SNOWSUIT

Ap

Every day for a week, draw what the weather looks like.
Then draw what you wear.

Monday

I am wearing _____ .

Tuesday

I am wearing _____ .

Wednesday

I am wearing _____ .

Thursday

I am wearing _____ .

Friday

I am wearing _____ .

Name _____

THOMAS' SNOWSUIT

Silly Sam wears the wrong clothes for the weather.
Cut and paste on the silly clothes Sam wears.

It is sunny but Silly Sam wears _____

_____.

It is rainy but Silly Sam wears _____

_____.

hat   swim fins/mask   tank top   sandals

swimsuit   umbrella   boots   coat

Name _____

40

THOMAS' SNOWSUIT

WRITING

Sy

Group Activity: Expand the postreading discussion. Discuss the clothing that all the children in the class wear in each season and every kind of weather. (List ideas on the board. Model writing sentences from the information.)

Ap/An

Pre-Writers: Draw pictures of what you would wear in hot weather, and in cold weather. Copy and complete these sentences:
"When I'm cold, I wear _____. When I'm hot, I wear _____."

Ap/An

Beginning Writers: List what you wear in hot weather and cold weather. Draw pictures.

Ap/An

Experienced Writers: Write about everything you wear when it is hot, and everything you wear when it is cold. Illustrate your work.

LANGUAGE ARTS

Ap/An

Where Can I Be?: Think about and describe different types of clothing. Ask other children to tell you where you would go comfortably in the described outfits.

MATHEMATICS

C

Zippers, Buttons, and Snaps: Determine the numbers of children who have zippers, buttons, snaps, Velcro, or other fasteners on their clothing. Translate your findings into mathematical equations such as the following:

$$\begin{array}{r} 20 \text{ zippers} \\ -\ 6 \text{ snaps} \\ \hline 14 \text{ more zippers than snaps} \end{array}$$

42 buttons + 20 zippers = _____

SOCIAL STUDIES

K/C

Where In The World?: Learn about climates in different parts of the world, and about the clothes people wear to adapt to their climates.

FINE ARTS

Sy/An

Sewing: Sew some simple garments to be worn in each season. Display them on a display table.

BRINGING RAIN TO KAPITI PLAIN

Summary: This rhythmic story tells of the drought-ridden Kapiti Plain, and how Ki-pat brings rain to it.

PREREADING DISCUSSION:

Why do we need rain? What does rain do for us? How do you think rain happens? (Discuss.) This is a story about the rain, Ki-pat, and Ki-pat's herd of cows in Africa. Listen to the rhythm of the words and learn about the make-believe way Ki-pat makes rain.

POSTREADING DISCUSSION:

Do you think clouds really break to spill out the rain? Do you think Ki-pat could make it rain with an arrow? (Discuss.) We're going to do an experiment that will show how rain is really made.

 EXPERIMENT:
What Makes It Rain?

You will need:
- A hot plate
- A pan of hot water
- A bowl of ice

1. Heat the pan of water on the hot plate. The heat **evaporates** the water, turning it into steam that rises.

2. Hold the bowl of ice over the steam of the hot water. As the hot steam meets the cold bowl, it will condense and make droplets of water. When the droplets get large enough, they fall like rain.

3. Draw the parts of the experiment that correlate with the actual rain cycle.

NOTE: When rain droplets are frozen, they become either snow or hail.

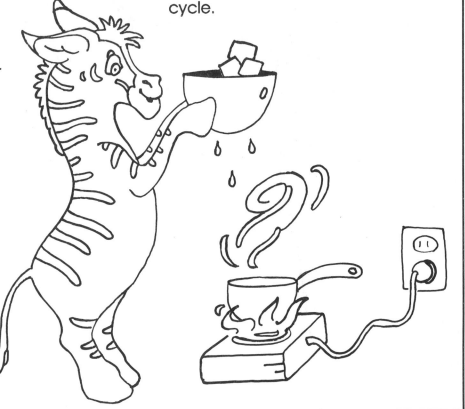

BRINGING RAIN TO KAPITI PLAIN

WHAT HAPPENS TO A MUD PUDDLE? – WHOLE GROUP

C

Discuss how mud puddles dry up after a rain. The water doesn't disappear, it **evaporates.** To illustrate this process, fill identical jars with identical amounts of water. Put a lid on one container and keep the other one open. Mark the water level of each jar every day. After a few days, the open jar will be empty because the water has evaporated.

WATER CONSERVATION – PAIRS OR COOPERATIVE GROUPS

C/An

Discuss different ways to conserve water. Some might be taking showers instead of baths, brushing teeth without the faucet running, or placing a plastic container of water in the toilet tank. (Keep track of the ways students conserve water.)

CHECKLIST	yes	no
shower	☐	☐
teeth w/o faucet	☐	☐
toilet container	☐	☐
gutter flooder	☐	☐

TOO LITTLE OR TOO MUCH RAIN – COOPERATIVE GROUPS OR WHOLE GROUP

Ev

Brainstorm ideas of what would happen if there were too little rain in your area. What would happen to the people and the animals? Work out a scenario and record it on a bulletin board. Then brainstorm what would happen if there were too much rain. Record that information, also.

ANIMAL MIGRATIONS – WHOLE GROUP

An

Study animal migrations in Africa, and in your own area. Chart migratory patterns on a map. Compare and contrast them. Discuss how these migrations would change if there were a drought.

RAIN GAUGE – PAIRS, COOPERATIVE GROUPS, OR WHOLE GROUP

C/Ap

Mark the side of a jar an inch from the bottom. Divide the inch measurement into four equal sections. Put it outside on a rainy day. Bring it in when the rain has stopped and measure the depth of the rain.

BRINGING RAIN TO KAPITI PLAIN

HOW TO MAKE THUNDER / LIGHTNING

You will need: A paper bag
                Two balloons

THUNDER:

1. Blow up the paper bag
    and hold it tight.

2. Hit it hard. It will pop. This is
    thunder.

WHAT HAPPENED?
Thunder is made when lightning heats
the air and moves it apart. When air
rushes back in it makes a loud noise.

LIGHTNING:

1. Blow up 2 balloons.

2. Rub them on the rug or drapes.

3. Hold them close together in a dark room.
    The spark you see is lightning.

BRINGING RAIN TO KAPITI PLAIN

WRITING

Sy **Group Activity:** Working as a class, chain the events of the story. What happened first, second, third, and so on?

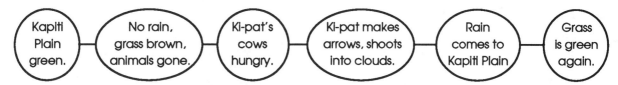

Ap **Pre-Writers:** Draw the Kapiti Plain. Copy and complete this sentence: "Kapiti Plain is _____ (green or brown) from _____(no or the) rain."

Ap **Beginning Writers:** Draw and write about one of the events in the chain.

Ap **Experienced Writers:** Write about any three events from the chain. Illustrate each of them.

LANGUAGE ARTS

An **Who Are You?:** In your small group, tell everything you know about an animal without mentioning its name. Ask the others to guess what it is.

Sy **Animal Books:** Choose a favorite animal and write everything you know about it in a book made in the shape of the animal.

Sy **Poetry:** Using the book for inspiration, write cumulative poems about the rain.

MATHEMATICS

An **Graphing:** Make a graph of the numbers of different animals pictured in the story.

SOCIAL STUDIES

K/C **All About Africa:** Learn about Africa.

An **Mapping:** Make a map of Africa and indicate where the animals live.

FINE ARTS

Ap/Sy **Diorama:** Construct a diorama that shows the rain cycle.

Sy **Masks:** Make cut-and-paste masks of African animals.

Sy **Papier Mâché:** Make your favorite African animals out of papier mâché.

HOUSEKEEPER OF THE WIND

Summary: Yula is the wind's housekeeper. Though they are friends, one day they get angry at each other and the wind unleashes his fury. In the end they lovingly resolve their differences and are friends again.

PREREADING DISCUSSION:

C/Ap

What kinds of things can the wind do? (List on board).

Example: blow in storms   make kites fly
          bring cool breezes   cause leaves to fall

In this story the Wind and a woman named Yula are friends. Listen for the things that the wind does.

POSTREADING DISCUSSION:

C

What kinds of things does the wind do in this story? (Circle correct responses and add new ones.)

Example: blows in storms   causes leaves to fall   makes gate creak
          makes kites fly   helps boats sail   brings rain
          brings cool breezes blows dry and hot   rattles windows

K/C **EXPERIMENT:**
Air That Moves Is Wind

You will need:
- Student reproducible page 48
- 1 balloon per child

1. Working with a partner, blow up your balloons and hold the ends shut. Is air moving in the balloon? Is there wind? (There isn't either.) Write down your answers.

2. With the help of your partner, hold the sides of your balloons and let go of the ends. Does the air move? Is there wind? (There is.) Write down your answers.

3. Discuss how wind can be a powerful force. Blow up your balloon again and let it go. Record what happens.

HOUSEKEEPER OF THE WIND

WIND WEATHER CENTER – INDIVIDUALS, PAIRS, COOPERATIVE GROUPS, OR WHOLE GROUP

Ap

Put together a weather center, using a wind sock and a pin-wheel to indicate how strong the wind is. Check your center daily to ascertain the direction and intensity of the wind.

KITE DAY – INDIVIDUALS, PAIRS, OR COOPERATIVE GROUPS

K/C

Make and decorate kites. Hold a Kite Day in your class. Measure how high the kites fly, how long they fly, best design and any other variables. Give prizes for the best kites in each category. Discuss how kites need wind to fly.

GOOD AND BAD WIND – PAIRS, COOPERATIVE GROUPS, OR WHOLE GROUP

Ev

Brainstorm a list of the many ways winds can help us and how they can hurt us.

MAKING AIR WORK – INDIVIDUALS OR PAIRS

Ap

Parachutes – Tie four pieces of string to a metal washer or some other weight. Tie the other ends of the strings to the four corners of a handkerchief. Throw your "parachute" into the air. Its fall will be slowed by the air it captures in its canopy. This is air resistance. (Discuss.) You can also gauge how fast the wind is blowing by how far it blows the parachute off course.

Glider – Make various paper airplanes and fly them. Determine which flies farthest, which flies straightest, which can "loop-the-loop," etc. Experiment with flying them with and against the wind.

HURRICANES / TORNADOES – COOPERATIVE GROUPS OR WHOLE GROUP

K/C

Study hurricanes and tornadoes — how they form, where they form, and the damage they can do. Learn how people can be prepared for them.

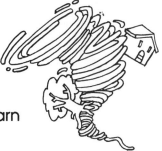

HOUSEKEEPER OF THE WIND

Ap

AIR THAT MOVES IS WIND

1. Blow up a balloon and hold it shut. Draw it.

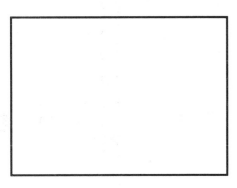

Is the air moving? _____

Is there wind? _____

2. Hold the sides of the balloon and let go of the end. Draw what happens.

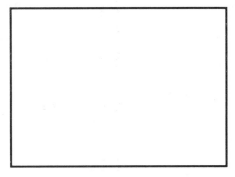

Is the air moving? _____

Is there wind? _____

3. Blow up the balloon and hold the end tightly. Then let it go. Draw what happens.

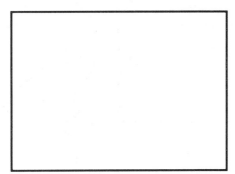

What did the wind do?

_____

_____

Name _____

HOUSEKEEPER OF THE WIND

Color and cut out the wind sock. Paste it together.

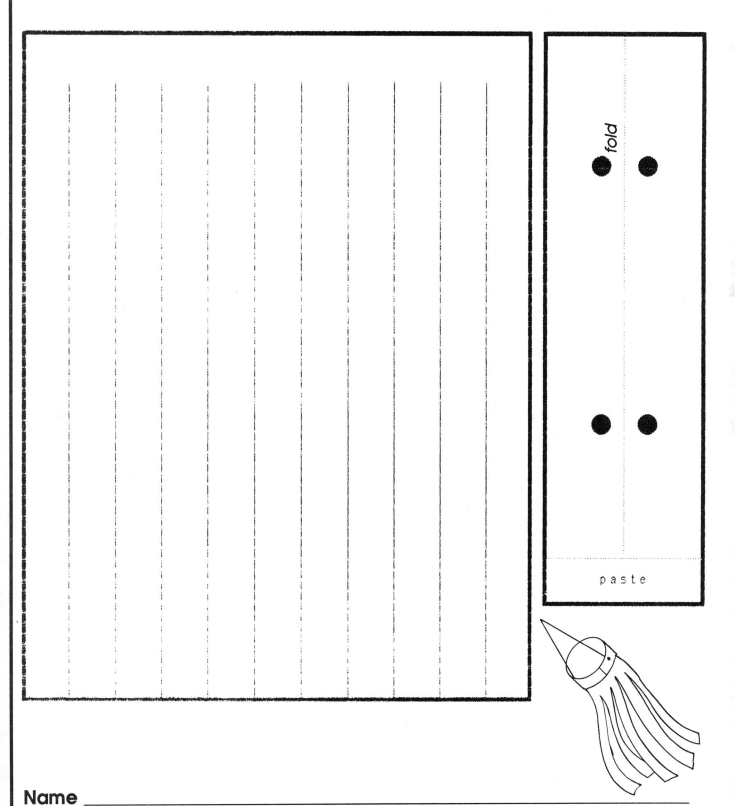

fold

paste

Name _____

HOUSEKEEPER OF THE WIND

WRITING

Sy **Group Activity:** Using information from the postreading discussion, and working as a group, dictate a chart story about things the wind can do.

Sy **Pre-Writers:** Draw something the wind can do. Copy and complete this sentence: "The wind can _____ ."

Sy **Beginning Writers:** Draw and write about two things the wind can do.

Sy **Experienced Writers:** Write about three things the wind can do. Illustrate your work.

LANGUAGE ARTS

An **Retell Story:** Act out and retell the story. (Encourage the children to add other endings or extend the story beyond the end of the book.)

MATHEMATICS

Ap **Measuring:** Have wind contests to see how far different objects will "fly." Use such things as feathers, tissue paper, cotton balls, paper plates, paper clips, pencils, etc.

SOCIAL STUDIES

Ev **Dealing With Anger:** Discuss how Yula and the wind acted when they were mad at each other, and how they made friends again. (Ask children how they deal with anger and how they say they're sorry.)

FINE ARTS

Sy **Wind Chimes:** Make wind chimes by tying nails, nuts, screws or other metal objects to a stick or coat hanger.

THE CLOUD BOOK

Summary: Cirrus, cumulus, and stratus clouds and their variations are introduced and pictured. Myths and sayings about clouds and weather are included.

PREREADING DISCUSSION:

Are all clouds shaped the same? What are some of the ways clouds look? (List on board.)

    Examples: fluffy

                like a blanket

                dark

                with long tails

Clouds have many different names. Listen to the story and watch for these kinds of clouds: cirrus, cumulus, and stratus.

POSTREADING DISCUSSION:

C

Cirrus, cumulus, and stratus clouds have different shapes. Describe these clouds.

CUMULUS	STRATUS	CIRRUS
fluffy	dark	long tails
puffy	like a blanket	high
like cauliflowers	low clouds or high fog	white
have flat bottoms		feathery
change shapes		

C/Ap **EXPERIMENT:**
Cloud In A Jar

You will need:
- Water
- Narrow-necked jar
- Hot plate
- Tea kettle
- Ice cubes

1. Pour a small amount of boiling water into the jar.

2. Cover the opening of the jar with ice cube(s) so that the steam won't escape.

3. Watch a cloud form and swirl.

A cloud is formed when warm air from the earth meets cold air in the atmosphere and condenses.

THE CLOUD BOOK

CLOUDS BRING MANY THINGS MURAL – COOPERATIVE GROUPS OR WHOLE GROUP

K/An Talk about the weather that different types of clouds bring: rain, hail, sleet, snow, cloudy days, etc. Record the types of clouds and their related weather. Make a class mural showing the different types of clouds.

CHART CLOUDS – INDIVIDUALS, PAIRS, COOPERATIVE GROUPS, OR WHOLE GROUP

Ap/An Chart clouds in the sky for a week. Draw them and identify them as cirrus, cumulus, or stratus. At the end of the week, graph your observations. Draw conclusions from your graph.

WEATHER MAP – WHOLE GROUP

Ap/An Watch videotaped weather reports and draw the cloud patterns shown in satellite pictures of the nation and your area.

WATCHING THE CLOUDS GO BY – INDIVIDUALS OR PAIRS

Sy Lie on your back and watch the clouds go by. Later, draw and record the different images and pictures you saw in the clouds.

CLOUDY THOUGHTS – PAIRS, COOPERATIVE GROUPS, OR WHOLE GROUP

An Discuss how clouds can be helpful and how they can be harmful. Record and illustrate your thoughts. Turn these ideas into a "CLOUD WORKS" poster, showing one example of helpfulness and harmfulness.

THE CLOUD BOOK

K

Cut out pictures of clouds and paste them next to their names.
Write something about each one.

Stratus

Stratus Clouds

_____

_____

Cumulus

Cumulus Clouds

_____

_____

Cirrus

Cirrus Clouds

_____

_____

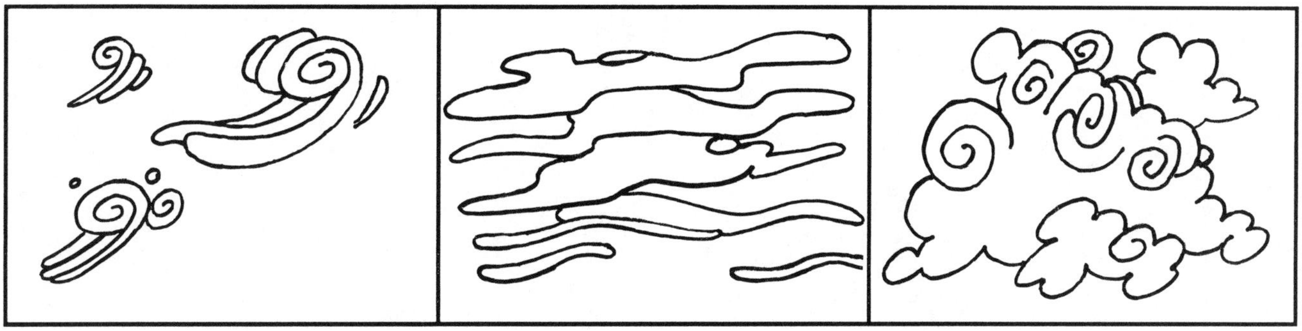

Name _____

THE CLOUD BOOK

WRITING

Sy   **Group Activity:** Discuss the different types of pictures all the children have seen in clouds. (List them on the board.)

Sy   **Pre-Writers:** Draw a picture you saw in a cloud. Copy and complete this sentence: "I saw _____ in a cloud."

Sy   **Beginning Writers:** Draw and write about a picture you saw in a cloud.

Sy   **Experienced Writers:** Write about a picture you saw in a cloud. Illustrate your work.

LANGUAGE ARTS

Sy   **Own Sayings:** Make up your own sayings about clouds.

Sy   **Cloud Stories:** Tell stories about clouds.

MATHEMATICS

K/C   **Cloud Math:** Count the clouds in the sky each day for a week. Work math problems, adding and subtracting the numbers.

SOCIAL STUDIES

An   **Global Map:** Make a map of the world. Draw cloud patterns covering it.

FINE ARTS

Sy   **Cotton Clouds:** Make representations of each type of cloud with cotton balls pasted on blue construction paper.

An   **Magazine Search:** Cut out magazine pictures showing the different types of clouds.

RAINBOW RIDER

Summary: A lonely Rainbow Rider looks for a friend in the desert. Only when his rainbow is made with his own tears does he truly find a friend.

PREREADING DISCUSSION:

Have you ever seen a rainbow? What colors were in it? (Discuss and write answers on board.) What do you think makes a rainbow? (Discuss.)

This is the story of Rainbow Rider, who makes rainbows. Look for the colors in the rainbow. What does Rainbow Rider use to make them?

POSTREADING DISCUSSION:

What colors were in the rainbow? (List words below on board. Have children circle correct answers and add others.)

green	pink
white	yellow
purple	blue
red	orange

What did Rainbow Rider make the rainbow from? (Answer: drops of water (his tears count as water drops too).)

K/C EXPERIMENT:
Make A Rainbow

A rainbow is made when light shines through water at an angle. The water bends the light so that each color shows.

You will need:
- A garden hose
- Clear glass of water
- Piece of white paper
- Pencil

GARDEN HOSE:
Point the hose away from you. Adjust the spray of water to a fine mist. Stand with your back to the sun. Move a little until you see a rainbow in the mist.

GLASS OF WATER:
Put the glass of water in direct sunlight. Lay the paper beside it so the sun shines through the glass and lands on the paper.

With your pencil, sketch around the rainbow. Color it.

RAINBOW RIDER

COLORS BACK TO WHITE – INDIVIDUALS, PAIRS, OR WHOLE GROUP

C/Ap

You will need: • 5-inch thick heavy paper plates • Scissors
• Heavy string • Crayons

1. Punch two holes close to the center of the paper plate.
2. Divide into six equal sections. Color three sections with bright primary colors.
3. Cut the raised rim off the paper plate so the plate will be flat and round.
4. Thread string through holes. Holding both ends, wind it up so string is twisted tight. Pull slightly so circle spins then slacken slightly to let it wind again. Continue pulling and slackening string.
5. Watch what happens to the colors. When the circle rotates, the eyes mix the colors together to form white.

COLORED LIGHTS – COOPERATIVE GROUPS OR WHOLE GROUP

Ap/An

You will need: • 3 flashlights • Red, blue, and yellow cellophane
Attach cellophane over the bulb ends of the flashlights. Darken the room and shine the flashlights so their colored light overlaps on a white surface. Record the resulting colors.

PRIMARY / SECONDARY COLORS – WHOLE GROUP

Sy/Ev

Learn the primary colors: red, blue, and yellow. Draw a picture using only those colors. Learn secondary colors: orange, green, and purple. Draw the same picture using secondary colors only. Compare the two pictures. Discuss the value of primary and secondary colors.

WASHABLE COLORS – WHOLE GROUP

C/Ap

You will need: • Dry laundry detergent • Food coloring
• Small paper cups, plastic spoons • Water

1. Fill cups almost to the top with detergent. Fill rest of the way with water.
2. Add 30 drops food coloring and stir until it becomes a thick mixture. (Supply only primary colors so students must mix to make secondary colors.)
3. Set in warm place to dry for 4 days. Peel off paper. Now you have crayons you can use in the bathtub (crayons can be wiped off bathtub sides).

COLOR OBSERVATION – INDIVIDUALS, PAIRS, OR WHOLE GROUP

Ap

(Find an area outside for students to sit and record everything they see that is each color of the rainbow.) Compare the most prevalent color and the least prevalent. Discuss why the one color was seen most. Would the color frequencies be different in the mountains? Desert? A snow scene?

RAINBOW RIDER

Color the rainbow.
Put the colors in the right places.

RAINBOW RIDER

3-D GLASSES

You will need:
- ½ file folder, or light cardboard
- Green cellophane
- Red cellophane
- Scissors
- Glue

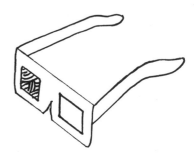

1. Trace glasses pattern on cardboard. Cut it out.

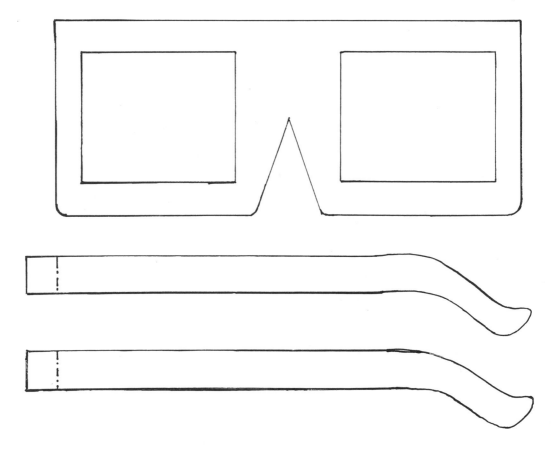

2. Glue glasses together. Glue red cellophane over one lens and green cellophane over the other.

ACTIVITIES: On another paper, draw what you see when you:
1. look through the green lens.
2. look through the red lens.
3. look through both lenses.

Name _____

RAINBOW RIDER

WRITING

`Sy` **Group Activity:** How would you be a friend to Rainbow Rider? (Write responses on board and model writing sentences from them.)

`Sy` **Pre-Writers:** Draw how you would be a friend to Rainbow Rider. Copy and complete this sentence: "To be a friend I would _____ ."

`Sy` **Beginning Writers:** Draw and write about how you would be a friend to Rainbow Rider.

`Sy` **Experienced Writers:** Write about what you would do to show Rainbow Rider you were his friend. Illustrate your work.

LANGUAGE ARTS

`Sy/Ev` **And Then What Happened?** Make up what happens after the end of the story. (If possible, record the children's ideas on a tape recorder and play it at the listening center.)

MATHEMATICS

`An` **Graphing:** Graph the numbers of children who are wearing different colors of the rainbow.

SOCIAL STUDIES

`Ev` **Color Feelings:** Discuss how certain colors make you feel.

FINE ARTS

`C/Ap` **Color Wheel:** Show how six colors of the rainbow result from the three primary colors red, blue and yellow.

`Ap` **Monochrome Picture:** Draw a picture using only one color. Discuss the limitations of monochrome and why colors are important.

THE TINY SEED

Summary: A tiny seed is blown on the wind. Many of the other seeds land where they won't grow. Will the tiny seed find a place to live?

PREREADING DISCUSSION:

Where do you think seeds come from? How do they travel? How do they grow? (Discuss.)

POSTREADING DISCUSSION:

C

What do seeds come from? How do they grow? (List answers on board.)

C/An **CONCEPT:**
Plant Cycle

You will need:
- Crayons
- Paper

1. Seeds are made by flowers. When the flowers get old, the seeds scatter and fall. (Teacher draws picture on board. Children draw on paper.)

2. Only some of the seeds find a good place to grow. When they do, they burst open a little and send down roots. (Draw.)

3. Then stems and leaves grow. (Draw.)

4. A flower forms on the stem. As it grows, seeds appear in the middle and the cycle starts again. (Draw.)

THE TINY SEED

SEED COLLECTION – INDIVIDUALS, PAIRS, OR COOPERATIVE GROUPS

`Ap/An`

Collect different kinds of seeds (pumpkin, beans, dandelion, sesame, peanuts, coconuts, pine cones, etc.). Categorize them, placing them in separate divisions in egg cartons. Discuss their similarities and differences. Glue one of each on a piece of construction paper. Label them.

PLANT SOME SEEDS – PAIRS, COOPERATIVE GROUPS, OR WHOLE GROUP

`C/Ap`

You will need:
- A clear glass jar
- Blotting paper (or very absorbent paper)
- Seeds (radish, bean, birdseed, etc.)
1. Place seeds between blotting paper and glass.
2. Moisten the paper and keep it moist.
3. Watch seeds sprout (within three or four days). Measure and observe the changes.

HOW SEEDS TRAVEL – PAIRS, COOPERATIVE GROUPS, OR WHOLE GROUP

`C`

Discuss how seeds travel by air, land, and water. Parachute seeds (like dandelions) travel on the wind. Some seeds (like coconuts) float on water. Others fall to the ground or are stored there by animals. Some weed seeds called burrs are carried on animal fur or on people's clothing.

p67

PLANT PRESSING – INDIVIDUALS, PAIRS, COOPERATIVE GROUPS, OR WHOLE GROUP

`C/Ap`

Pick a selection of plants complete with roots and press each plant between two sheets of waxed paper under a heavy book. Once pressed and dry, paste or arrange them on paper and label the parts.

PLANT / SEED OBSERVATION – INDIVIDUALS, PAIRS, OR COOPERATIVE GROUPS

`Ap/An`

Observe a mature patch of weeds and select one or two specific plants and their seeds to draw. Speculate on how the seeds might travel and make a notation of it.

THE TINY SEED

SEED TREAT FOR BIRDS

You will need:
- Milk carton from school
- Scissors
- String
- Birdseed

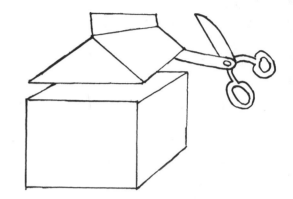

1. Cut the top off a clean milk carton.

2. Poke holes in each side. Tie string through the holes.

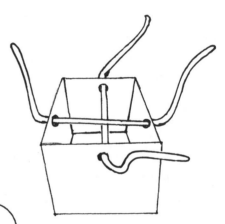

3. Pour in birdseed.

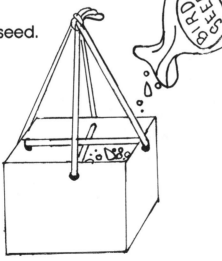

4. Hang your feeder on a tree. Watch the birds come and eat.

Name _____

THE TINY SEED

WRITING

Ap **Group Activity:** Working as a class, dictate a chart story using information gained from the postreading activity.

C **Pre-Writers:** Draw one of the steps in the plant cycle. Copy and complete the appropriate sentence from the chart story.

C **Beginning Writers:** Draw two steps in the plant cycle. Write about them.

Sy **Experienced Writers:** Write about the steps in the plant cycle. Illustrate your work.

LANGUAGE ARTS

Sy **Seed Travels:** Children tell or write stories about the travels of a seed. (Tape record them and play them at the listening post.)

C/An **Plant Descriptions:** Observe a plant and describe it (writing or speaking) to a partner. The partner draws the plant from the description.

MATHEMATICS

Ev **Pea Pod Estimation:** The teacher will provide pea pods. Estimate how many peas are in each pod. You must base your estimates on observable phenomena. Once estimates are made, open pods and count peas. Graph the results.

C/Ap **Measuring:** Make a trail mix out of different edible seeds.

SOCIAL STUDIES

An **Mapping:** Draw detailed maps showing where the tiny seed went in the story.

An/Ev **Useful Plants:** Discuss how plants and seeds are useful to us.

FINE ARTS

Sy **Seed Art:** Make pictures or designs by gluing seeds on paper, cardboard, or wood.

Sy **Imaginary Plant:** Draw or paint your own imaginary plants and their seeds.

THE PLANT SITTER

Summary: Tommy is plant-sitting for neighbors on vacation. He cares for the plants so well that the house becomes a jungle. Using his head, he solves the problem.

PREREADING DISCUSSION:

K/C

What kinds of things do plants need in order to live? (Discuss.)

This is a story about Tommy, who takes care of his neighbors' plants. See what he does to take care of them.

POSTREADING DISCUSSION:

C

What did Tommy do to take care of the plants? What do plants need to survive? (List on board.)

> Water
> Light
> Cutting back (pruning)
> A good place to grow

C/Ap **EXPERIMENT:**
What Do Plants Need To Survive?

You will need:
- Student reproducible page 66
- Seeds (radish, mustard, or birdseed)
- 3 flower pots
- Soil

1. Plant the same number of seeds in each soil-filled flower pot. Label the pots #1, #2, #3. Set them on the window sill.

2. Make the following notations on reproducible page 66.
   Pot #1: No water or sunlight (Cover it with a box.).
   Pot #2: Give water, but no sunlight.
   Pot #3: Give water and sunlight.

3. Each day for a week, observe the three pots and make drawings of the results. At the end of the week, come to a conclusion about the experiment.

THE PLANT SITTER

PLANTS SEEK LIGHT – INDIVIDUALS, PAIRS, COOPERATIVE GROUPS, OR WHOLE GROUP

`C/Ap`

You will need:
- A healthy plant
- Tape
- Scissors
- Shoebox

1. Cut one end out of the shoebox and cut out a window in the lid.
2. Tape the lid on firmly. Turn the box on end and place it over the plant with the box's window facing away from the light.
3. Take off the box and check the plant daily. The leaves and flower will have turned toward the box's window, its only source of light.

PLANTS GROW FROM DIFFERENT THINGS – COOPERATIVE GROUPS OR WHOLE GROUP

`K/C`

Discuss how plants grow from seeds, bulbs, roots, and cuttings. Cultivate common plants that grow from each of these sources.

Seeds: Bean
Bulbs: Onion or tulip / daffodils
Cuttings: Geraniums
Roots: Carrot top or sweet potato

HOW PLANTS DRINK WATER – PAIRS, COOPERATIVE GROUPS, OR WHOLE GROUP

`K/C`

You will need:
- Glass of water
- Red or blue food coloring
- Stalk of celery with top leaves

1. Put 10-12 drops of food coloring in water.
2. Place celery stalk in colored water.
3. Observe it every 30 minutes and note changes. (Celery ribs will turn color of water as water moves up the stalk.)

PLANT RESEARCH – INDIVIDUALS, PAIRS, OR COOPERATIVE GROUPS

`C/Ap`

Research a specific plant and report on it by:
- bringing in a sample.
- mapping where it grows.
- drawing a poster showing how we use it.

LEAF COLLECTION – INDIVIDUALS, PAIRS, COOPERATIVE GROUPS, OR WHOLE GROUP

`An`

Bring in leaf samples from all the different plants the children have at home. Categorize and draw them. See if you can match them to the flowers they make.

THE PLANT SITTER

WHAT PLANTS NEED TO SURVIVE

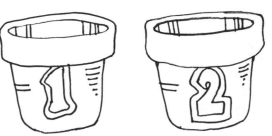

Draw what the sprouting seeds look like each day.

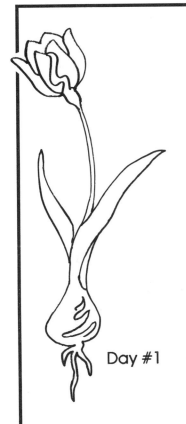

	Pot #1	Pot #2	Pot #3
Day #1			
Day #2			
Day #3			
Day #4			
Day #5			

Which potted plant grew the best? _____

Why? _____

Name _____

THE PLANT SITTER

Ap/An

Cut out the book and fold it.

Draw and write about how to care for plants.

THE PLANT SITTER

WRITING

`Ap` **Group Activity:** Using the information from the postreading activity, dictate sentences about what plants need to grow. (Write them on the board.)

`Ap` **Pre-Writers:** Draw the things plants need to grow. Copy and complete this sentence: "Plants need _____ and _____ to grow."

`Ap` **Beginning Writers:** Draw and write about the things plants need to grow.

`Ap` **Experienced Writers:** Write a paragraph about what plants need in order to grow. Illustrate your work.

LANGUAGE ARTS

`Ev` **Read And Retell:** The teacher will read *The Carrot Seed* by Ruth Krauss to the class. Once you are familiar with the story, retell it and act it out in small groups.

`An` **Sequencing:** Divide a piece of paper into four parts. Draw and write the steps in planting and caring for a plant. Cut them apart and arrange them in sequence.

Example:

plant seeds	water seeds
keep in light	plant grows

MATHEMATICS

`C` **Money Math:** In the story, Tommy got paid 2 cents a day for each plant he cared for. Create math problems to figure out how much money Tommy made.

Example: Tommy had one plant for six days. How much money did he make?
Tommy had three plants for four days. How much money did he make?

`An` **Symmetry:** Look at different leaves from plants. Discuss how some are the same on both sides (symmetric) and some aren't (asymmetric).

SOCIAL STUDIES

`An/Ev` **Helpful Plants:** Take a "plant walk" around the neighborhood. Note the different kinds of plants and discuss how they help people.

FINE ARTS

`Sy` **Leaf Pressing:** Collect a number of different leaves. Lightly coat them with paint and press them onto paper to make leaf prints.

A TREE IS NICE

Summary: A tree is nice for climbing, and provides leaves to roll in, bird nests, shade, and so many other things. But planting a tree of your own is even better.

PREREADING DISCUSSION:

K/C

What do trees do for us? (Discuss.)

This is a story about trees and how they are nice. Listen as we learn of the many things they provide.

POSTREADING DISCUSSION:

C

What do trees do for us? (List on board. Encourage children to think of their own ideas.)

C/Ap **CONCEPT:**
Tree Parts And What They Do

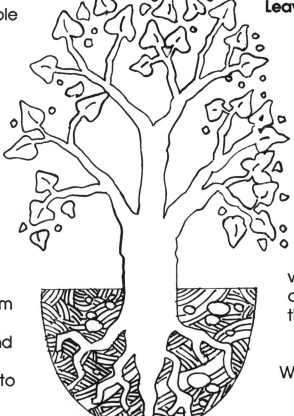

You will need:
- Student reproducible page 71
- Pencils
- Crayons

1. The teacher will draw a tree on the board as you draw one on your paper.

2. Trees have 4 parts. Each part has a different function:
   Roots - Get water and nutrients from the soil.
   Trunk - Supports and protects tree. Carries nutrients to all its parts.

Limbs - Are extensions of the trunk. Support leaves.
Leaves - Collect sunlight and carbon dioxide and give off the oxygen we breathe.

3. Draw a line on your paper from the word to the correct tree part.

4. Trees help clean the air. They make *oxygen.* (Write the word on the board so children can write it on their papers.)

We breathe *oxygen.* We need trees to live.

A TREE IS NICE

DO LEAVES BREATHE? – COOPERATIVE GROUPS OR WHOLE GROUP

C/Ap

You will need:
- 4 clear plastic glasses
- 2 pieces of cardboard
- Scissors
- Leaf

1. Put water into two drinking glasses.
2. Cut a hole in each piece of cardboard and place one on each water-filled glass.
3. Put a fresh leaf through one hole so its stem is in the water and top it with an inverted glass. Set up the other apparatus the same way but without the leaf.
4. The inside of the leaf glass will develop water droplets; the other won't. This proves that leaves give off moisture.

DECIDUOUS AND EVERGREEN – PAIRS, COOPERATIVE GROUPS, OR WHOLE GROUP

C/An

Learn about the difference between deciduous and evergreen trees. (Deciduous trees lose their leaves in the fall; evergreen trees don't.) Collect leaves of deciduous and evergreen trees. Compare and contrast them.

READING TREE RINGS – PAIRS, COOPERATIVE GROUPS, OR WHOLE GROUP

C/Ap

Observe cross-sections from a tree. Count the tree rings to determine the age of the tree. Notice any irregularities in spacing between rings; a narrow ring indicates a year without much rain or snowfall. Make note of other interesting markings.

PLANT A TREE POSTER – INDIVIDUALS OR PAIRS

Ap/Sy

Design posters encouraging people to plant trees. Post them around the community, in supermarkets, malls, etc. This is an excellent activity for Arbor Day. (Contact local nurseries or your reference librarian for sources of free tree seedlings for the children to plant.)

TREE SEEDS – INDIVIDUALS, PAIRS, COOPERATIVE GROUPS, OR WHOLE GROUP

C/An

Collect a variety of tree seeds:

acorns	nuts
fruit seeds	pine cones, etc.

Match them to the trees they produce. Notice similarities and differences. Plant them to see if they'll grow.

A TREE IS NICE

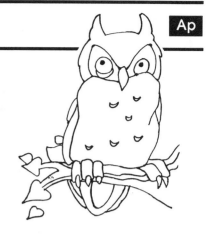

Ap

TREE PARTS AND WHAT THEY DO

Draw a tree.

Leaves
Take in light and
carbon dioxide.
Give off oxygen.

Trunk
Supports and
protects the tree.

Limbs
Hold the leaves.

Roots
Get water from the ground.

Trees help clean the air. They make _____.

We breathe _____.

We need trees for _____.

Name _____

A TREE IS NICE

Select a tree.

Draw your tree:

Its leaf looks like this:

Do a bark rubbing:

List the animals you see or hear in your tree. _____

_____

What does your tree smell like? _____

What does your tree feel like? _____

On the back of this paper, show in a drawing how you will care for your tree.

Name _____

A TREE IS NICE

WRITING

C/Ap

Group Activity: Discuss the various ways trees are nice. Expand upon the postreading list. (Encourage children to give many examples to complete the sentence: "Trees are nice because _____ .")

Ap/Sy

Pre-Writers: Draw a picture to show one way that trees are nice. Copy and complete this sentence: "Trees are nice because _____ ."

Ap/Sy

Beginning Writers: Draw pictures to show two ways that trees are nice. Copy and complete this sentence: "Trees are nice because _____ ."

Ap/Sy

Experienced Writers: Write about three or more ways in which trees are nice. Illustrate your work.

LANGUAGE ARTS

C

Read / Listen Tree Stories: Listen to these tree stories, then retell them in your own words. (Tape such books as *The Giving Tree* and *Johnny Appleseed* so children may listen to them and retell on their own.)

Ap/Sy

Shape Book: Write stories about trees in tree-shaped books.

MATHEMATICS

An/Ev

Estimation: Estimate the numbers of trees in the schoolyard and neighborhood block. Take a tree walk to count the trees.

SOCIAL STUDIES

Ap

Tree Use: Learn about the different ways people use trees (for shade, lumber, camping in forest, etc.).

Ev

Good / Bad: Discuss the good and bad points of cutting down trees to use as lumber.

FINE ARTS

Ap/Sy

Bark Rubbings: Make bark rubbings of various trees in the areas.

Ap/Sy

Leaf Prints: Make leaf impressions in plaster of paris and paint them to hang on the wall.

Sy

Tree Collages: Make colllages out of seeds, pods, leaves, needles, and bark of various trees.

A PET FOR MRS. ARBUCKLE

Summary: Mrs. Arbuckle wants a pet. After advertising for one, she takes a ginger cat and travels around the world to interview the animals who applied.

PREREADING DISCUSSION:

Ap

What kinds of things would you look for in a pet? What kinds of things would you need to give a pet? (Discuss.)

POSTREADING DISCUSSION:

C/An

What were some things Mrs. Arbuckle did want and did not want in a pet? (List on board.)

K/Ap **CONCEPT:**
What Pets Need

Taking care of a pet is a big responsibility. Pets need attention every day. They need:
- Food
- Shelter (a place to stay)
- Love

There are many pets to choose from and they all need different foods

and shelters. (List animals and discuss the food and shelter they need.)
- birds
- fish
- gerbils
- cats
- dogs
- rats and mice
- guinea pigs
- hamsters
- horses
- snakes and lizards

You can show them love in different ways, too:
- petting them
- scratching their ears, stomachs, under chin
- talking to them nicely
- spending time with them

A PET FOR MRS. ARBUCKLE

CHOOSING A PET – PAIRS, COOPERATIVE GROUPS, OR WHOLE GROUP

`Ap`

Discuss the kinds of things that need to be considered when choosing a pet. Some questions to ask yourself are:
- Do you have a large yard?
- Do you have time for a pet?
- Does your family want a pet, too?
- How much will it cost?

Generate a realistic list of questions and include it in a "Choosing A Pet" pamphlet made by the class.

PET STORE FIELD TRIP – COOPERATIVE GROUPS OR WHOLE GROUP

`C/An`

Take a trip to a pet store and record all the material available for each animal. Cooperative groups can each have the responsibility of drawing and writing everything they see having to do with a certain kind of pet. Discuss.

INSECT HOTEL – INDIVIDUALS, PAIRS, OR COOPERATIVE GROUPS

`C/Ap`

You will need: • Jar with a lid   • Hammer and nail
Punch holes in the lid with the hammer and nail. Catch an insect to keep as a short-term pet and put it in the jar with a leaf and twig (or whatever its shelter is) and some food. Observe and record its behavior, how it eats, and how it uses its shelter. Let it go after a while. (Teach that releasing it is being responsible for the well-being of wildlife.)

PET SCHEDULE – COOPERATIVE GROUPS OR WHOLE GROUP

`Ap/An`

Each day have students share their pet duties from that morning and the afternoon before (activities such as feeding, walking the dog, changing litter box, playing with animal). Keep a daily chart to reinforce that having pets requires responsibility.

PRETEND A PET – INDIVIDUALS, PAIRS, OR COOPERATIVE GROUPS

`Ap/Sy`

This is a great activity, especially for children who don't or can't have pets. Design a pet, draw it on lightweight cardboard, color it, and cut it out. Then make a small shelter for it out of a small box or milk carton. (The pet can then be named and talked or written about.)

75

A PET FOR MRS. ARBUCKLE

Sy

Draw a pet you'd like to have. Draw what
it would eat, where it would stay, and how
you would love it.

My pet is a _____ .

It eats _____ .   It lives _____ .   I will love it by _____

_____ .

Name _____

© 1992 by Incentive Publications, Inc., Nashville, TN.

A PET FOR MRS. ARBUCKLE

An

How many people in your class have these pets?
Fill in the graph.

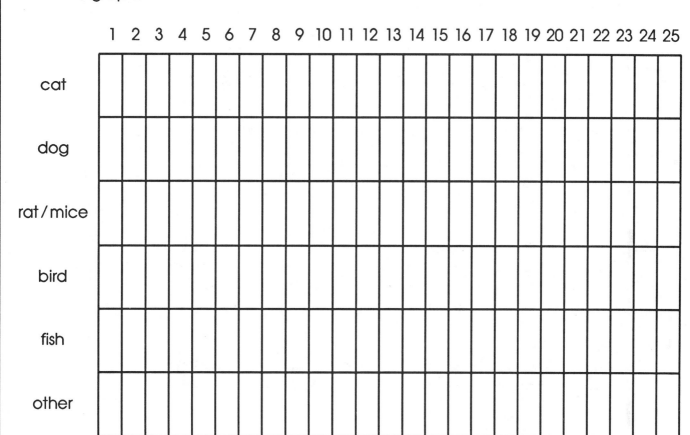

	1	2	3	4	5	6	7	8	9	10	11	12	13	14	15	16	17	18	19	20	21	22	23	24	25
cat																									
dog																									
rat/mice																									
bird																									
fish																									
other																									

1. What pet do most of your classmates have? _____ .

2. Nobody has these pets: _____ .

3. The least owned pet is _____ .

4. _____ people have cats.

5. _____ people have dogs.

6. What else can you tell from the graph? _____

_____

_____

Name _____

A PET FOR MRS. ARBUCKLE

WRITING

`Sy` **Group Activity:** Use information gained in postreading discussion. What would you want to say if you advertised for a pet? (List ideas, then model writing sentences from them. Encourage originality in children's writing.)

`Sy` **Pre-Writers:** Draw the kinds of things you want in a pet. Copy and complete this sentence: "I want a pet that is _____ ."

`Sy` **Beginning Writers:** Draw and write about the kinds of things you want in a pet.

`Sy` **Experienced Writers:** Write about the different qualities you want in a pet. Illustrate your work when you're done.

LANGUAGE ARTS

`Ap/An` **Who Am I?** Make up riddles that tell what an animal looks like, eats, and what its shelter is. Others try to guess what the animal is. This can also be done in pantomime.

MATHEMATICS

`C` **Weight And Measure:** Weigh classroom animals and other animals that children can safely bring in cages or containers. Measure their lengths, too. Weigh and measure the appropriate amounts of food and water each animal needs for a day.

SOCIAL STUDIES

`C` **Pet In The Family:** Discuss how each child's family takes care of its pet.

`K/C` **Pets Around The World:** Learn about the animals Mrs. Arbuckle visited and the countries they come from.

FINE ARTS

`Ap` **Birdfeeder:** Make birdfeeders out of common household items (e.g., tuna cans, milk and egg cartons, etc.).

`Ap` **Modeling Clay:** Model favorite pets out of clay.

`Ap` **Diorama:** Make a diorama showing what a pet eats, drinks, and where it lives.

THE DAY JIMMY'S BOA ATE THE WASH

Summary: A girl recounts her class's field trip to the farm. It is boring " . . . until the cow started crying." Then it dissolves into a comedy of mishaps.

PREREADING DISCUSSION:

What are some of the animals you would expect to see on a field trip to the farm? (Discuss.)

POSTREADING DISCUSSION:

What are the farm animals you saw in the book? (Discuss.)

 **CONCEPT:**
What We Get From Farm Animals

Farm animals are very important. We get much of our food and clothing from them. Here's a list of the products they produce:

Cows ➤ Milk ....cottage cheese • cheese • cream • sour cream • yogurt
➤ Beef..........steak • hot dogs • hamburger • roasts • liver

Pigs ➤ Pork ....sausage •
pork chops •
bacon • lard

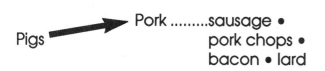

Chicken ➤ Eggs ....scrambled,
etc. • use in
cooking
➤ Chicken

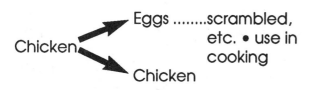

Sheep ➤ Wool.......sweaters •
blankets •
coats • socks

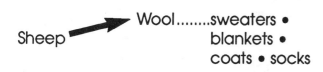

THE DAY JIMMY'S BOA ATE THE WASH

FARM ANIMALS AND THEIR YOUNG – PAIRS, COOPERATIVE GROUPS, OR WHOLE GROUP

`K/C`
Study the babies of farm animals and their life cycles.
(Have the children draw and illustrate each one.)

FARM CHORES – PAIRS, COOPERATIVE GROUPS, OR WHOLE GROUP

`Ap/An`
Discuss the care and feeding of farm animals. (What
kinds of chores might the children have to do if they lived on a farm? Have
them make a schedule of what their day would be like if they
lived on a farm.)

COWS	PIGS
Food: hay and grass	Food: corn and slop
Care: milk twice each day / feed	Care: need pen / feed
Chores: milk and feed cows	Chores: feed pigs
CHICKENS	SHEEP
Food: grain	Food: grass
Care: need chicken house / feed	Care: large field to graze
Chores: feed chickens, gather eggs	Chores: feed & shear sheep

TRACK THAT MEAL – PAIRS, COOPERATIVE GROUPS, OR WHOLE GROUP

`Ap/An`
Trace the ingredients of popular foods (pizza, cheeseburgers, breakfast sand-
wich, etc.) back to the farm and /or to the animals that made them possible.

PIZZA	BREAKFAST SANDWICH	PANCAKES
crust – wheat	biscuit / muffin – wheat	wheat
sauce – tomatoes	egg – chicken	milk / butter – cow
cheese – cows	cheese – cows	eggs – chicken
pepperoni – cows, pigs	bacon – pigs	

RACING RESEARCH – INDIVIDUALS, PAIRS, OR COOPERATIVE GROUPS

`K/Ap`
Do some fun research activities to learn about one of the
farm animals. The teacher will supply lots of magazines
and picture books. Activities can include the following:
1. Find a picture of a baby animal and the adult animal.
   Draw it or cut it out and write its name.
2. Cut out pictures of three things we get from the animal.
3. List two new things you learned about the animal.
4. Make a model of the animal's home on a farm.
5. What would your day be like if you were the animal?
   Be prepared to act it out or tell about it.

MAP YOUR OWN FARM – INDIVIDUALS, PAIRS, COOPERATIVE GROUPS, OR WHOLE GROUP

`An`
Discuss the different features of a farm — chicken house,
barn, pigsty, farmhouse, animals, roads, fields, etc. (Have children map out their
own farms.)

THE DAY JIMMY'S BOA ATE THE WASH

Draw some of the things we get from farm animals.

Name _____

THE DAY JIMMY'S BOA ATE THE WASH

Draw the farm animals on the farm.

Name _____

THE DAY JIMMY'S BOA ATE THE WASH

WRITING

Ap/An **Group Activity:** Chaining – Make a chain of what would happen if Jimmy took his new pet pig to the zoo.

Ap/An **Pre-Writers:** Draw one thing that would happen if Jimmy took his pig to the zoo. Copy and complete this sentence: "The pig would _____ ."

Ap/An **Beginning Writers:** Draw and write a sentence about what would happen to the pig.

Ap/An **Experienced Writers:** Write your own chain of events. Illustrate it.

LANGUAGE ARTS

Sy **Animal Shape Books:** Cut out a shape book to resemble the outline of a farm animal. Write stories about the animals.

Sy **Funny Field Trip:** Sitting in a round-robin circle, make up portions of a crazy field trip to the farm or the zoo. Each person gets to tell one thing that happens and the next person adds to it. (Write down what children say, making a class book.)

MATHEMATICS

K/C/Ap **Farm Math:** Generate mathematical equations using farm animals and events from the story.

> Examples: The snake scared four pigs and six children. How many animals did the snake scare?
>
> $4 + 6 = 10$
>
> Pigs got on the bus and ate ten sandwiches, two apples, and five bags of chips. How many things did they eat?
>
> $10 + 2 + 5 = 17$

SOCIAL STUDIES

Ev **Farms Are Important:** Discuss the many ways farms are important to the community. They provide food and jobs to many people (farmers, truck drivers, store clerks, etc.).

FINE ARTS

Ap/An **Switch 'Em Change 'Em:** Cut out magazine pictures of animals, then cut them in halves or thirds. Mix them up and create crazy animals. Name them and tell about them.

FISH IS FISH

Summary: Two friends, a minnow and a tadpole, grow up and become different animals. As a fish and a frog they learn to appreciate their different worlds.

PREREADING DISCUSSION:

An

How are fish and frogs alike and different? (Discuss.)
This is a story about a fish and a frog. See how they are alike and different.

POSTREADING DISCUSSION:

An

How are fish and frogs alike and different? (Discuss. List on board.)

ALIKE	DIFFERENT
Live in water	Frogs hop / fish can't
Swim	Frogs on land / fish not
Smooth Skin	

C **CONCEPT:**
Fish And Amphibian Life Cycles

You will need:
  • Student reproducible
    page 86

FISH: Fish live in the water all of the time. They hatch from eggs and become tiny fish called larva or fry. The fry grow bigger and bigger and become fish.

FROGS: Frogs are *amphibians.* That means they live in water and on land. They hatch from eggs and become tadpoles. As the tadpoles grow, they get hind legs, then front legs, then their tails get shorter. Finally they become frogs that can hop on land and swim in the water.

FISH IS FISH

AQUARIUM – COOPERATIVE GROUPS OR WHOLE GROUP

`C`

You will need: • Large glass container • Plants (plastic or real)
• Gravel • Minnows and tadpoles
The teacher will help the class construct an aquarium. Observe it daily. Draw and record the changes the minnows and tadpoles go through every day or so.

FROG JUMP – INDIVIDUALS, PAIRS, OR COOPERATIVE GROUPS

`Ap`

Catch and "train" a frog. Learn to care for it, building a comfortable terrarium with some classmates. (Frogs can eat fish food, lettuce, insects and bits of hardboiled egg.) On a prescribed day, hold a contest to see how far each frog can go in three jumps. The only rule is that you cannot touch the frog to make it jump.

MORE FISH AND AMPHIBIANS – PAIRS, COOPERATIVE GROUPS, OR WHOLE GROUP

`K`

Learn about other kinds of fish and amphibians. Fish have a **backbone** and **gills** and live in the water. Interesting fish include:

Sharks Sea horses Eels Flying fish
Manta ray Piranha Puffer fish Goldfish

Amphibians have four limbs, breathe through gills, and live where it is very moist. Interesting amphibians include:

Frogs Mudpuppies Newts
Salamanders Toads

Alone or in groups, research a favorite fish or amphibian and report on it.

POND LIFE – COOPERATIVE GROUPS OR WHOLE GROUP

`K/Ap`

You will need: • Samples of pond water • Eyedroppers
• Magnifying glasses • Waxed paper
• Microscope (if available)
Using eyedroppers, drop small amounts of pond water onto waxed paper and observe it through magnifying glasses. Draw and record what you see.

A DAY IN THE LIFE – INDIVIDUALS, PAIRS, COOPERATIVE GROUPS, OR WHOLE GROUP

`Ap`

After learning about different fish and amphibians, select your favorite and make a fish or amphibian puppet. Have it act out and explain what it is and what its typical day might be like.

FISH IS FISH

LIFE CYCLES

Color, draw, and label the life cycle of a fish.

_____   larva or fry   fish

Color, draw, and label the life cycle of a frog.

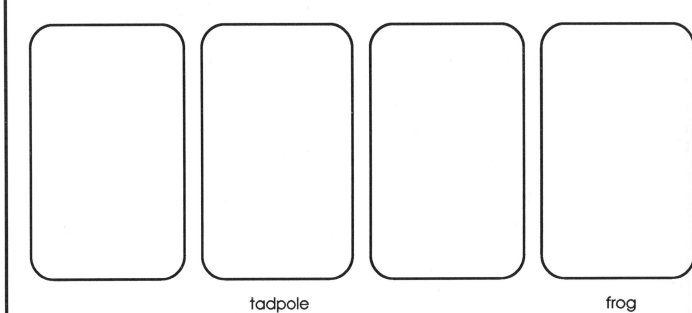

_____   tadpole   _____   frog

Name _____

FISH IS FISH

Ap

HOW TO MAKE A TERRARIUM

You will need:
- Jar with lid
- Sand and dirt
- Charcoal
- Small plants
- Small frog or amphibian

1. Put sand and charcoal on the bottom of the jar.

2. Put dirt on top of sand.

3. Plant some plants. Water them.

4. Punch holes in the lid for air.

5. Put a small frog or other amphibian in the jar. Watch it. Let it go when you are finished.

NOTE: Frogs eat lettuce, mealyworms, flies, or small pieces of cooked egg.

Name _____

FISH IS FISH

WRITING

Sy/Ev — **Group Activity: What If?** If you were the fish, what do you think an elephant would look like? (Discuss.)

Sy — **Pre-Writers:** Draw how the elephant might look to the fish. Copy and complete this sentence: "The elephant has _____ ."

Sy — **Beginning Writers:** Draw and write about how the fish might think an elephant looks.

Sy — **Experienced Writers:** Write a description of an elephant from the fish's point of view. Illustrate your idea.

LANGUAGE ARTS

K/C — **Read About It:** Encourage children to check out and read books about fish and amphibians.

Ap — **Who Am I Riddles:** In a small group, make up riddles about specific fish and amphibians. Others guess what it is.

MATHEMATICS

Ap — **Measuring Frog Jumps:** Use rulers and yardsticks to measure how far a frog jumps in three jumps. (This can be used in conjunction with the "Frog Jump" Science Activity.)

Ev — **Estimating Fish Scales:** (Bring a frozen fish into class.) Estimate the number of scales the fish has, then count them.

SOCIAL STUDIES

Ev — **How They Are Helpful:** Learn how fish and amphibians are helpful to humans. (Fish supply food to us and amphibians eat insects.)

FINE ARTS

Ap — **Watercolor/Crayon Wash:** Draw pictures of pond life (fish and amphibians) with crayon on white paper. Then create a watercolor wash of blue, brown, and green paint in the appropriate areas.

Ap — **Fish Prints:** Make prints of dead fish using printer's ink and a roller or paint and paintbrush. Roll or brush a thin layer of ink or paint on the fish and lay paper on it to make a print.

ANIMALS BORN ALIVE AND WELL

Summary: A charming book of rhymes about the characteristics of mammals found on land and sea.

PREREADING DISCUSSION:

Have you ever seen baby kittens or puppies? What covered their bodies? What did they breathe? Did they nurse from their mother? (Discuss.)

Animals who are born alive, have fur or hair, and nurse are called mammals. Listen for different kinds of mammals in this book.

POSTREADING DISCUSSION:

C/Ap

What were some of the mammals mentioned in the book? (List on board.) Can you think of some other animals who are mammals?

K **CONCEPT:**
What Makes A Mammal?

Mammals are animals who:

1. Are born alive.

2. Have fur or hair.

3. Breathe air.

4. Nurse (get milk from their mother).

Mammals live on land and in the sea. They live where it is hot and where it is cold. They can be pets, live in a zoo, or in the wild. They come in all sizes.

ANIMALS BORN ALIVE AND WELL

CATEGORIZATION – PAIRS OR COOPERATIVE GROUPS

`An`

Draw pictures of many different mammals on uniform pieces of paper. Working in a small group, categorize them in many ways (land / water, zoo / pets / wild, size, color, etc.). Keep track of the different categories and share them.

MAMMAL WATCH – COOPERATIVE GROUPS OR WHOLE GROUP

`C`

Go on a "mammal walk" around your schoolyard or neighborhood. Draw and list all the mammals you see. Share in groups and brainstorm lists of other mammals that might live nearby.

DESIGN A SHELTER – INDIVIDUALS, PAIRS, OR COOPERATIVE GROUPS

`Ap`

Choose a favorite mammal and learn about it, then model a shelter for it. Write or tell why you chose your shelter and how it helps your mammal.

WHO AM I? – COOPERATIVE GROUPS OR WHOLE GROUP

`Ap/An`

Write "Who am I?" riddles about specific mammals. Present the riddle to the group and ask the others to guess what it is.
　　　Example: I am large, white and furry.
　　　　　　　 I live in the ice and snow.
　　　　　　　 I eat fish and seals. Who am I? **(Polar Bear)**
This is also a fun pantomiming activity.

MAMMAL IN A SHOEBOX – INDIVIDUALS, PAIRS, OR COOPERATIVE GROUPS

`C/Ap`

Learn everything you can about a favorite mammal. Put artifacts and information in a shoebox and share it. The box can contain:
- Collage of pictures showing mammal, its babies, habitat, etc.
- Examples of its food, habitat, fur, paw prints, etc.
- Audio tape from the mammal's point of view telling about it.
- Puppet / model of mammal.

ANIMALS BORN ALIVE AND WELL

An

Draw animals who are mammals
and animals who are **not** mammals.

— MAMMALS —   — NOT MAMMALS —

because _____

because _____

because _____

because _____

because _____

because _____

Name _____

91

ANIMALS BORN ALIVE AND WELL

Make up your own mammal.

My mammal is called a _____ .

Its body is covered with _____ .

Its habitat is _____ .

It sleeps _____ .

Its babies are called _____ .

Name _____

92

ANIMALS BORN ALIVE AND WELL

WRITING

C **Group Activity:** (Generate a list of mammals. Ask children to dictate sentences about mammals and write them on the board.)

K/C **Pre-Writers:** Draw a mammal. Copy and complete the sentences: "Mammals are born alive. A _____ is a mammal."

C **Beginning Writers:** Draw and write about two mammals.

C **Experienced Writers:** Write about what makes an animal a mammal. Give three examples of mammals. Illustrate your work.

LANGUAGE ARTS

C **Listen, Listen:** Record favorite stories abut mammals and place the tapes at the listening post.

C **Read About It:** Read books about mammals for silent reading.

MATHEMATICS

K **Listen, Listen:** Record favorite stories about mammals and place the tapes at the listening post.

An **Graphing:** Graph the types of mammals seen on the mammal walk.

SOCIAL STUDIES

Ap/An **Maps:** Map where all the mammals mentioned in the book live.

Sy **Mapping:** Map where the class's imaginary mammals live.

FINE ARTS

Ap **Diorama:** Construct dioramas of specific mammals and their habitats.

Ap **Mobiles:** Make mobiles out of pictures and artifacts of favorite mammals, their homes, habitat, and young.

ANIMALS SHOULD DEFINITELY NOT WEAR CLOTHING

Summary: Animals might wear clothes upside down, wear them in the wrong places, get them wet or . . . who knows what else? This delightful book proves that animals already have the right coverings.

PREREADING DISCUSSION:

What kinds of "clothes" or coverings do animals have? What do you think would happen if they started to wear clothes the way we do? (Discuss.)

This is a fun story about why animals should definitely *not* wear clothing. Listen and watch for what each animal is wearing and the problems he or she has.

POSTREADING DISCUSSION:

C

What were some of the animals wearing in the story? (List on board.)

K **CONCEPT:**
Animals Already Have The Clothes They Need

Animals don't really wear clothes, but they all have the coverings they need. They are:
- fur
- skin
- hair
- scales
- feathers

Fur helps keep animals warm. Dogs, cats, wolves and bears all have fur. Most animals who live where it is cold have fur.

Elephants, pigs, frogs, and people all have **skin**.

Animals with **hair** don't live in really cold places. Giraffes, cows, horses and monkeys have hair.

Scales cover fish and snakes. When scales get wet they can help the animal move.

Birds have **feathers**. Feathers are light, keep birds warm, and help them fly.

ANIMALS SHOULD DEFINITELY NOT WEAR CLOTHING

TAKE A LOOK – COOPERATIVE GROUPS OR WHOLE GROUP

`K/Ap`

You will need: • Magnifying glass
• Frozen fish
Observe the scales of the fish and other things about the fish's covering. What does it feel like, look like, smell like? Draw and write what you observe.

TERRARIUM – INDIVIDUALS, PAIRS, OR COOPERATIVE GROUPS

`K/Ap`

Make a terrarium out of a large jar. Punch holes in the top, put in dirt, plant small plants, and add a reptile or amphibian (frog or lizard). Observe these animals who have skin. Learn how it helps them.

COLLECTION – COOPERATIVE GROUPS OR WHOLE GROUP

`An`

The teacher will put together a collection of different scales, feathers, fur, hair, and skin. Discuss and write about their similarities and differences. Discuss things we make out of animal coverings.

ANIMAL WALK – PAIRS, COOPERATIVE GROUPS, OR WHOLE GROUP

`K/Ap`

Take a walk about the neighborhood and make a record of the different animals you see and the body coverings they have. Graph your results.

BIRDS OF A FEATHER – PAIRS, COOPERATIVE GROUPS, OR WHOLE GROUP

`K`

Study the many different kinds of birds, where they live, and what they eat. Give a report about a specific bird. Construct a model or diorama of their bird's habitat and tell about it.

DESIGN AN ANIMAL – INDIVIDUALS, PAIRS, COOPERATIVE GROUPS, OR WHOLE GROUP

`Ap/Sy`

Come up with an idea for an original animal and make it. Glue or sew on its covering. Make up the place it lives and what it eats, and tell all about it.

ANIMALS SHOULD DEFINITELY NOT WEAR CLOTHING

C

Draw an animal that has
each kind of covering.

FUR

A _____ has fur.

SKIN

A _____ has skin.

SCALES

A _____ has scales.

FEATHERS

A _____ has feathers.

Name _____

ANIMALS SHOULD DEFINITELY NOT WEAR CLOTHING

What if you had feathers or scales?
What would be good about it?
What would be bad?

Sy/An

FEATHERS
If I had feathers I would look like this.

Feathers are
GOOD because _____

_____

_____

Feathers are BAD because _____

_____

_____

SCALES
If I had scales I would look like this.

Scales are GOOD because _____

_____

_____

Scales are BAD because _____

_____

_____

Name _____

ANIMALS SHOULD DEFINITELY NOT WEAR CLOTHING

WRITING

Ap/An

Group Activity: Elaborate on postreading discussion. Think of some other animals. What problems would they have with clothes? (List on board. Model writing sentences from information. Encourage originality in students' writing.)

Sy

Pre-Writers: Draw an animal wearing clothes. Copy and complete this sentence: "A(n) _____ should never wear _____ ."
　　　　　　　　　(animal)　　　　　　　　　　　　　　　　　(clothing)

Sy

Beginning Writers: Draw and write about an animal wearing clothes.

Sy

Experienced Writers: Write about two animals and the problems they would have wearing clothes. Illustrate your story.

LANGUAGE ARTS

Sy

Class Books: Working in small groups, write and illustrate reasons animals should definitely *not* wear clothing. (Have children select animals that are not in the book.) Compile into class books that can be read during silent reading.

MATHEMATICS

K/Ap

Add 'Em Up: Count up the numbers of certain types of clothing in the book (e.g., hats, coats, ties, sweaters, etc.). A graph can be made of the results.

An

Zoo Categorization: After a visit to the zoo, draw animals on cards. Working in small groups, categorize the animals.

SOCIAL STUDIES

K

Clothes From Different Countries: Learn about the different types of clothing people wear around the world.

FINE ARTS

Sy

Cut-And-Paste Clothes: (Provide children with pictures of animals.) Using the pictures of animals provided, design clothing for the animals and paste it on.

CHICKENS AREN'T THE ONLY ONES

Summary: Chickens aren't the only animals born from eggs. Many different animals are — reptiles, amphibians, fish, and birds.

PREREADING DISCUSSION:

What animals can you think of that are born from eggs? (Discuss.)

This book is about many of the animals that come from eggs. Watch and listen for them.

POSTREADING DISCUSSION:

What are some of the animals mentioned that come from eggs? (Draw or list on board.)

Animals who come from eggs are called *oviporous.*

C **CONCEPT:**
Whose Eggs Are Whose?

You will need:
• Student reproducible page 101
Eggs have many different shapes and sizes.

CHICKENS AREN'T THE ONLY ONES

WHY EGGS AREN'T ROUND – INDIVIDUALS, PAIRS, OR COOPERATIVE GROUPS

Ap

You will need: • Chicken eggs
• Plastic spoons
Discuss the fact that most eggs laid on land aren't
round (this is so they won't roll away). Have an egg
race during which you try to roll eggs in a straight
line. Roll the eggs on a flat surface and notice they
naturally go in circles. This clearly illustrates why
eggs are shaped the way they are.

WHERE ARE THEY – COOPERATIVE GROUPS OR WHOLE GROUP

K/An

Learn about the places different animals lay their eggs:
Water (fish, amphibians)
Leaves (insects)
Dirt / sand (reptiles)
Nests (birds)
Spun sacs (spiders)
Draw or bring in samples of different
eggs. Children can study one of
these groups and report on them.

INCUBATE CHICKEN EGGS – WHOLE GROUP

K

Incubate chicken eggs in the class-room. Contact local chicken suppliers for
the loan of an incubator. Keep a daily log of your observations. Be sure to
record the daily temperature, and the date and time that each egg hatches.
Point out the special "egg tooth" which unborn chickens and other egg-born
animals have to help them break out of their shells.

EGG CAMOUFLAGE – COOPERATIVE GROUPS OR WHOLE GROUP

K/Ap

You will need: • Banty hen eggs of different colors and markings
• Pictures or examples of other bird eggs
Though bird eggs are fragile, they have natural
protection from predators because of their markings
that serve as camouflage. Discuss where the birds
would lay their eggs so that they wouldn't show.
Draw an egg's markings and the area where the
egg would be laid so it couldn't be seen.

PARTS OF A CHICKEN EGG – PAIRS, COOPERATIVE GROUPS, OR WHOLE GROUP

K

Study and observe the parts
of a chicken egg.

CHICKENS AREN'T THE ONLY ONES

WHOSE EGG IS WHOSE?

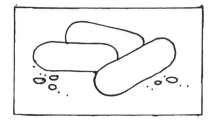

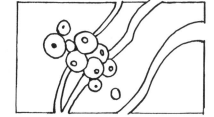

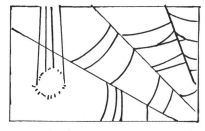

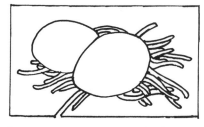

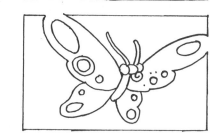

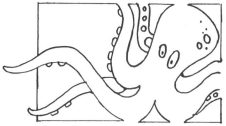

Name _____

CHICKENS AREN'T THE ONLY ONES

WRITING

Ap **Group Activity:** Write a chart story about all the different animals who lay eggs. Include the concept that every animal that lays an egg is *oviporous.*

Ap **Pre-Writers:** Draw an animal that comes from an egg. Copy and complete this sentence: "A _____ comes from an egg."

Ap **Beginning Writers:** Draw and write about two animals who come from eggs.

Ap **Experienced Writers:** Write about two or three animals who come from eggs. Illustrate your story.

LANGUAGE ARTS

K/C **Read About It:** Read stories of animals who come from eggs. ("Little Red Hen," etc.)

Ap/Sy **Diary:** Tape record a diary of an animal as it hatches from an egg.

MATHEMATICS

An **Size Comparison:** Children compare sizes of many different eggs and rank them from smallest to largest.

K **Measuring:** Measure the circumferences of different eggs.

SOCIAL STUDIES

Ap **How People Use Eggs:** Discuss the many ways people use eggs.

K **Ukrainian Easter Eggs:** Learn about the Ukrainian people and the ornately decorated eggs they make.

FINE ARTS

Ap **Pantomime:** Pantomime hatching from an egg.

Ap **Egg Sensations:** Make replicas of eggs, wrapping papier mâché around balloons. Paint them and cut them in half. Each child should draw the animal who would hatch from the egg and put the drawing inside the egg replica.

THE SNAIL'S SPELL

Summary: A child shrinks to the size of a snail and explores the world of the garden.

PREREADING DISCUSSION:

If you were a snail, what other animals and plants would you see in a garden? (Discuss.)

This is a story about becoming a snail in a garden. Look carefully for the other animals and plants that live there.

POSTREADING DISCUSSION:

What plants and animals were in the garden? (List on board.)

 EXPERIMENT:
Snail Watch

You will need:
- Student reproducible page 105
- 1 snail for each child (or pair of children)
- Rulers
- Garden or vegetable area to observe snail

1. Draw your snail.
2. Touch the snail gently. Record what it feels like and what it does.
3. Observe how the snail moves. Measure how far it goes in one minute. Draw what it leaves behind.
4. Record what it does, what it eats, and how it eats.

THE SNAIL'S SPELL

SNAIL RACES – INDIVIDUALS, PAIRS, OR COOPERATIVE GROUPS

Ap

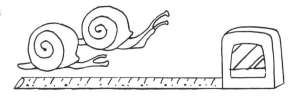

You will need: • Snails
• Tape measure
• Stopwatch or
other timing device

Race the snails against one another by measuring how far each snail travels in one, two, or five minutes.

INVERTEBRATES – PAIRS, COOPERATIVE GROUPS, OR WHOLE GROUP

K

Learn about two other related invertebrates: slugs and worms. Study their eating habits and how they are helpful and harmful to humans. Catch and observe snails, slugs, and worms, then compare and contrast their behaviors.

TASTE SNAIL FOOD – COOPERATIVE GROUPS OR WHOLE GROUP

Ev

Take a closer look at the garden foods represented in the book's illustrations. Think of other food grown in a garden and taste them all. Graph the results of the taste test.

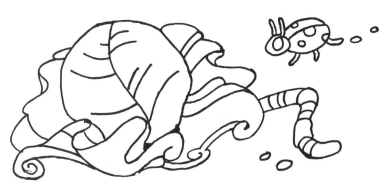

SNAIL'S EYE VIEW – INDIVIDUALS OR WHOLE GROUP

Ev

With painted snail-shell boxes on your backs, get down on the ground and become snails the way the child in the story did. Using your arms as feelers, move about at a snail's pace to get a snail's eye view of the world.

IT'S A SMALL WORLD – INDIVIDUALS, PAIRS, OR COOPERATIVE GROUPS

K/Ap

You will need: • Paper
• Pencils
• Magnifying glasses

Each child or group will stake out a small patch of earth (about a foot square) and observe the movement of insects and anything else that happens there in a five- to ten-minute time period. Draw and write down observations.

THE SNAIL'S SPELL

Ap/An

SNAIL WATCH

1. Draw your snail.

2. Touch your snail gently. What did it feel like?

_____

What did the snail do
when you touched it?

3. How does the snail move? _____

How far does it go in a minute? _____

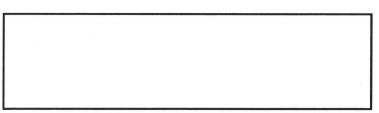

Draw what it leaves behind
when it moves.

4. What did the snail eat?

On the back of this paper, draw and write down other things your snail did.

Name _____

THE SNAIL'S SPELL

WRITING

Ev   **Group Activity:** Generate ideas about how the child in the story felt when he became a snail. (Encourage class to use descriptive words. List phrases on board.)

Sy/Ev   **Pre-Writers:** Draw how it would feel to be a snail. Copy and complete this sentence: "It would feel _____ to be a snail."

Sy/Ev   **Beginning Writers:** Draw and write about how it would feel to be a snail.

Sy/Ev   **Experienced Writers:** Write two sentences about how it would feel to be a snail. Illustrate your work.

LANGUAGE ARTS

Sy   **Amazing Shrinking Children :** Make up stories about shrinking to a small size, what it would feel like, and what you would do.

Ap   **Talk At A Snail's Pace:** Practice talking very slowly, as slowly as a snail moves.

MATHEMATICS

K/Ap   **Measuring:** Using a ruler for measuring, find things that are 2 inches long (as long as the snail in the story).

SOCIAL STUDIES

An   **Interview:** Get many people's reactions to snails. Make a chart of their reactions.

FINE ARTS

Ap   **Clay Models:** Construct clay models of snails. Put the models in a garden.

UNDER THE MOON

Summary: A mother mouse teaches her child how to tell the meadow from the woodlands by the smells and sounds around them.

PREREADING DISCUSSION:

What animals, sights, and sounds are in a meadow? In the woods? (Discuss.)
This is a story about a little mouse who is learning the difference between the meadow and the wood. Listen carefully and look at the pictures to find the animals, sights, and sounds of each place.

POSTREADING DISCUSSION:

What are the animals, sights, and sounds of the meadow? The woods? (List on board.)

 CONCEPT:
Animals Of Meadow And Woodlands

You will need:
- Student reproducible page 109
- Scissors
- Paste
- Construction paper
- Crayons

1. Draw pictures of woodlands and meadow on construction paper.

2. Discuss how a greater variety of animals lives in the woods because the woods provide better protection and more places to hide than does the meadow.

3. Go back through the book to study pictures of woodland and meadow animals.

4. Cut out pictures of appropriate animals on reproducible page and paste them on your construction paper drawings of woods and meadow.

UNDER THE MOON

RECONSTRUCT MEADOW / WOODLAND HABITAT – COOPERATIVE GROUPS OR WHOLE GROUP

Ap/An

On a large, flat surface construct a meadow and woodland habitat using dirt, twigs, moss, pebbles, grass seed, etc. Children can model animals out of clay and put them in their appropriate places in the habitat.

PREDATORS AND PREY – PAIRS, COOPERATIVE GROUPS, OR WHOLE GROUP

K/Ap

Learn about which animals are predators and which are prey in the meadow and woodlands habitats. Discuss the abilities both predators and prey must have to survive:

PREDATORS	PREY
good eyesight	quickness
sharp claws	agility
ability to move fast	good eyesight / hearing

MOUSE BOOK – INDIVIDUALS, PAIRS, COOPERATIVE GROUPS, OR WHOLE GROUP

Ap

Research mice by observing mouse behavior in the classroom. (Put findings into a class book colorfully illustrated by the children. Make it available for silent reading times.)

SOUNDS AND SMELLS OF HOME – INDIVIDUALS, PAIRS, OR COOPERATIVE GROUPS

Ev

Close your eyes and pay attention to the sounds and smells of the classroom, the school grounds, and your home. Write down descriptions. Discuss their similarities and differences. What causes them to differ?

ENDANGERED SPECIES – COOPERATIVE GROUPS OR WHOLE GROUP

K/Ap

Learn about endangered species in meadow and woodland environments:
- Bats (gray, Indiana, Ozark big-eared, Virginia big-eared)
- Spotted owl
- Fox (Northern swift, San Joaquin Kit)
- Falcons, peregrines (all)

For information, ask for "Endangered and Threatened Wildlife and Plants" from U. S. Dept. of Interior, U. S. Fish and Wildlife Service, 1849 C Street NW, Washington, D.C. 20240. Write to these organizations to learn how to protect endangered species:

The Audubon Society
950 3rd Avenue
New York, NY 10022

National Wildlife Federation
1400 16th Street NW
Washington, D.C. 20036

UNDER THE MOON

ANIMALS OF WOODS AND MEADOW

Draw pictures of the woods and meadow on other paper.
Color and cut out the animals shown below.
Paste them on your pictures.

Name _____

UNDER THE MOON

Go outside and watch an animal.
Draw and write down the sights, sounds, and smells found where it lives.

Draw the animal.

What can it see?	What can it hear?	What can it smell?
It can see	It can hear	It can smell

Name _____

UNDER THE MOON

WRITING

Ap/Sy

Group Activity: Expand upon the Postreading activity by having children describe the animals, sights, and sounds of each place (woodlands and meadow).

      Example: Furry, soft mice
                    Tangy berries
                    Bubbling water, etc.

Encourage children to use their descriptive phrases in their own writing.

Ap/Sy

Pre-Writers: Draw something from the meadow and something from the woods. Copy and complete these sentences: "The meadow has _____ . The woods have _____ ."

Ap/Sy

Beginning Writers: Draw and write about something from the meadow and something from the woods.

Ap/Sy

Experienced Writers: Write about two things from the meadow and two things from the woods. Use describing words. Illustrate your work.

LANGUAGE ARTS

Ev

Smells And Sounds: Describe the smells and sounds you like and dislike. Then explain why.

An

Environmental Sounds: Listen to commercial environmental tapes of woodlands and meadows. Pick out the sounds you recognize.

MATHEMATICS

K/An

Count And Graph It: Go through the book and keep a tally of how many different animals are pictured. Graph your results.

SOCIAL STUDIES

Ev

Roads: Discuss how roads are helpful and harmful to people and animals.

FINE ARTS

Ap

Moon Wash Drawings: Using crayons, draw the meadow at night with a large moon overhead. Paint over your picture with dark blue watercolors. The paint will dissipate over the crayon wax and give the effect of night.

Ap

Predator And Prey Pantomime: Pantomime the interrelationships between predators and prey in the woods and in the meadow.

RAIN FOREST

Summary: Animals of the rainforest live peacefully until a machine comes and starts tearing out the trees.

PREREADING DISCUSSION:

What do you know about the rainforest? What animals live there? (Discuss.)

This story is about the animals living in the rainforest and what happens when their home is in danger. Listen, and watch for the different animals and what happens to the rainforest.

POSTREADING DISCUSSION:

What animals live in the rainforest? (List on board.) How is their home in danger?

 CONCEPT:
Importance Of Rainforests

You will need:
- Student reproducible page 114
- Crayons

1. The teacher will show you where you are on the map. (Approximate.) Mark it with a small "x."

2. Rainforests exist in the tropical belt of the earth centered around the equator. Draw a red line along the equator.

3. Color the land in the tropical belt green. This is where the earth's rainforests are. They are called rainforests because it rains there almost every day.

4. Many trees and plants grow in the rainforest and they give off most of the oxygen in our atmosphere. Oxygen is what we need to breathe so we can survive. Color the atmosphere around the earth light blue.

5. Trees in the world's rainforests are being cut down. When they are gone, we all lose.

6. You can help save the rainforest by writing letters to important people, eating food grown in rainforests, and not buying things made of rainforest wood.

RAIN FOREST

ANIMALS OF THE RAINFOREST – INDIVIDUALS, PAIRS, OR COOPERATIVE GROUPS

C/Ap

Research an animal of the rainforest. Report findings by:
* explaining what a day for this animal would be like.
* drawing pictures.
* bringing examples of its food, shelter, etc.

SOIL EROSION – COOPERATIVE GROUPS OR WHOLE GROUP

K

You will need: • 2 shallow trays of dirt
                     • Grass seed
1. Plant grass seed in one tray of dirt, water it, and allow it to sprout and become well rooted. Leave the other tray of dirt bare.
2. Tilt each tray at a steep angle. Pour water over each. The grass seedlings will hold soil in place; dirt from the other tray will erode.

RAINFOREST FOOD TASTING – INDIVIDUALS, PAIRS, COOPERATIVE GROUPS, OR WHOLE GROUP

Ev/An

Taste foods from the rainforest:
* papaya   • Brazil nuts
* mango   • cashews
* bananas   • passion fruit and guava juices

Record texture, color and taste of each.

SAVE THE RAINFOREST – INDIVIDUALS, PAIRS, OR COOPERATIVE GROUPS

Ap

Make posters, bumper stickers, and buttons that tell about the importance of rainforests and how to save them. Encourage other students to wear buttons and place bumper stickers on family cars.

Devise a 30-second radio ad and approach local stations to air it as a public service announcement. You'll be surprised at how receptive these stations can be to such an idea.

RAINFOREST TERRARIUM – PAIRS, COOPERATIVE GROUPS, OR WHOLE GROUP

Ap

You will need: • Jars with lids • Charcoal
                  • Hammer   • Potting soil
                  • Nails   • Small moisture-loving plants
1. Use hammer and nail to pound a few holes in jar lids.
2. Place charcoal bits at bottom of jar to prevent soil from souring.
3. Put soil in jar and plant many plants. Water well and put lid on.
4. Observe how moisture and plant respiration cause droplets to adhere to sides of jar. This is evidence of the important air-cleaning work the rainforest does.

RAIN FOREST

RAINFORESTS ARE IMPORTANT

Follow the directions.

1. Put an X where you live.
2. Draw a red line along the equator.
3. Color the land in the tropical belt green.
4. Color the atmosphere light blue.

YOU CAN SAVE THE RAINFOREST:
- Write letters.
- Eat food grown there.
- Don't buy rainforest wood.

Name _____

RAIN FOREST

RAINFOREST TRAIL MIX

- 2 cups cashews

- 1 cup Brazil nuts

- $1/4$ cup dried mango and / or papaya (you can find these where food is sold in bulk bins)

- $1/2$ cup dried bananas

- $1/2$ cup chocolate chips

1. Mix everything together.

2. Eat and enjoy!

RAIN FOREST

WRITING

Ap

Group Activity: Write a letter about the threatened rainforest. (Model writing letter for students.) Send it to:

> International Union of Conservation of Natural Resources
> 1110 Muges
> Vand, Switzerland

K

Pre-Writers: Copy and complete this letter format.

"Dear People,
  Please save the rainforest.
    Your Friend,

Draw a picture to go with it.

   _____ "

Ap/Sy

Beginning Writers: Write a letter about saving the rainforest. Illustrate your work.

Ap/Sy

Experienced Writers: Write a letter about saving the rainforest. Draw a picture to accompany it.

LANGUAGE ARTS

Ev

Animal's Point Of View: Tell, write, and listen to rainforest stories made up from the animal's point of view.

C

Read About It: Read other books about the rainforest and the animals who live there.

MATHEMATICS

An

Graph Rainforest Foods: After tasting foods from the rainforest, graph the number of students who liked each one.

SOCIAL STUDIES

An

Mapping: Map South America's rainforests before and after the clear-cutting of trees began.

K/C

What Can I Do? Show other students how they can help the rainforest in a powerful way by:
- not buying things made of exotic hardwoods (teak, mahogany, etc.).
- eating food produced by rainforest trees.
- planting trees in your own area to replenish oxygen in atmosphere.

FINE ARTS

Ap

Wet Paper Art: Make paintings or chalk drawings on wet paper to give the effect of strong colors used in story illustrations.

Sy

Puppet Show: Construct animal puppets to tell stories about the rainforest.

HOW TO HIDE A POLAR BEAR

Summary: Mammals and their natural camouflages are wonderfully illustrated and set to rhyme.

PREREADING DISCUSSION:

Why are polar bears white? Why do zebras have stripes? (Discuss.)

This book shows how some mammals' markings help them blend into their surroundings. Watch to see where each animal hides.

POSTREADING DISCUSSION:

Why are polar bears white? Why do zebras have stripes? What markings do other animals have and where do they hide? (List on board.)

An   CONCEPT:
Types Of Animal Camouflage

You will need:
- Student reproducible page 119
- Pencils
- Crayons
- *How To Hide A Polar Bear* and other books with animal pictures if available

1. Generate lists of animals that use spots, stripes, or solid colors as camouflage. Use as many reference sources and picture books as possible.

Examples:

SPOTS
   deer
   leopard
   giraffe

STRIPES
   zebra
   tiger

ONE COLOR
   polar bear
   lion
   sloth

2. Draw pictures of animals using each type of camouflage.

HOW TO HIDE A POLAR BEAR

GOING UNDERCOVER – INDIVIDUALS, PAIRS, COOPERATIVE GROUPS, OR WHOLE GROUP

Ap

Discuss the kinds of camouflage that would work best for hiding in different areas of schoolyard or neighborhood. (Children dress up in various outfits to blend into surroundings. Class chooses which outfit works best in which environment.)

DIORAMAS – INDIVIDUALS, PAIRS, OR COOPERATIVE GROUPS

Ap

Construct 3-D Dioramas of animals hiding in their natural surroundings. (NOTE: As a fun addition to this activity, have children create their own original animal and give it markings that will help it blend into its surroundings.)

CAMOUFLAGE VESTS – INDIVIDUALS OR PAIRS

Ap

You will need: • 1 large paper bag per child
                 • Scissors
                 • Crayons

1. Cut paper bag to make a vest. (Turn inside out if bag has store logo on it.)
2. Color and decorate with the camouflage markings of a favorite animal.

STRANGE ANIMALS – INDIVIDUALS, PAIRS, COOPERATIVE GROUPS, OR WHOLE GROUP

K

Learn about strangely-camouflaged animals (insects that look like leaves, bark and twigs; fish that look like rocks or the sandy bottom . . .).

MURAL – INDIVIDUALS, PAIRS, OR COOPERATIVE GROUPS

Ap

Construct a class mural of mammals, their markings, and where they hide.

HOW TO HIDE A POLAR BEAR

K/C

ANIMAL
CAMOUFLAGE

Draw and write the names of animals that use each kind of camouflage.

Name _____

© 1992 by Incentive Publications, Inc., Nashville, TN.

HOW TO HIDE A POLAR BEAR

WRITING

Ap/Sy

Group Activity: Using information from postreading activity, dictate sentences about each animal in the book. (Encourage children to add other animals if they can.)

C

Pre-Writers: Draw an animal and where it hides. Copy an appropriate sentence from the chart story.

Sy

Beginning Writers: Draw and write a sentence about an animal and where it hides.

Sy

Experienced Writers: Write about two animals and where they hide. Illustrate your work.

LANGUAGE ARTS

K/C

Author! Author! Read these other books by Ruth Heller on this issue:

How To Hide An Octopus
How To Hide A Butterfly
How To Hide A Grey Tree Frog
How To Hide A Crocodile
How To Hide A Whip-poor-will

MATHEMATICS

Ev

How Many Spots? How Many Stripes? Estimate how many spots / stripes animals had in the book. Check it out by counting them.

SOCIAL STUDIES

Ap

People Camouflage: Discuss how and why people use camouflage (war, hunting, camping). Discuss the times when people don't want to blend into surroundings (walking, biking at night, etc.).

FINE ARTS

Ap

Camouflage Masks: Construct masks of various animals with camouflages.

THE DESERT IS THEIRS

Summary: The dry, hot desert has many plants and animals living on it. They share it and live along with the Desert People.

PREREADING DISCUSSION:

What is the desert like? What kinds of plants and animals live there? (Discuss.)

This is a story about the people, plants, and animals that live in the desert. Listen and watch for them.

POSTREADING DISCUSSION:

What are the plants and animals that live in the desert? (List on board.)

C/Ap **CONCEPT:**
Desert Plants And Animals

You will need:
- Student reproducible page 123
- Crayons
- Scissors
- Paste
- Piece of paper

1. Discuss how the desert is hot and dry. Animals and plants have adapted to that environment.

Plants:
- thick skins
- no leaves
- store water
- thorns and stickers
- long roots

Animals:
- many nocturnal to avoid heat of day.

2. Color and cut out plants/ animals of the desert and paste them on your paper.

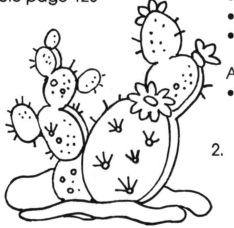

THE DESERT IS THEIRS

ANIMAL TRACKS – INDIVIDUALS, PAIRS, OR COOPERATIVE GROUPS

Ap

Learn about the tracks various desert animals leave in the sand.

DESERT TERRARIUM – PAIRS, COOPERATIVE GROUPS, OR WHOLE GROUP

K

You will need: • Rectangular glass terrarium or aquarium
• Sandy soil
• Desert plants (small cacti and succulents)
• Desert animals (small lizard or snake)

Plant plants in sandy soil and introduce the animal. Keep the animal properly fed and the plants watered periodically. Observe your tiny desert ecosystem and compare to your own environment.

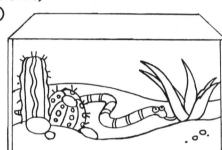

TASTE DESERT FOODS – INDIVIDUALS, PAIRS, OR COOPERATIVE GROUPS

Ev/An

Taste food from the desert: corn, squash, beans, pumpkin seeds, sunflower seeds, cactus fruit, and flesh.

Record the texture and flavor of each food. (Graph the reactions of the class.)

DESERT PLANTS EFFICIENCY – COOPERATIVE GROUPS OR WHOLE GROUP

K

You will need: • A small succulent
• A small leafy plant
1. Place each plant in similar light conditions and water them with equal amounts of water.
2. Observe plants each day without watering them and note changes.

DAY IN THE LIFE – INDIVIDUALS, PAIRS, OR COOPERATIVE GROUPS

Ev

Research specific desert animals by:
• constructing a diorama or model of their home or den.
• describing a typical day in the life of the animal from the animal's point of view (what they eat, how they hunt, care for their young, etc.).

DESERT ANIMALS – INDIVIDUALS, PAIRS, COOPERATIVE GROUPS, OR WHOLE GROUP

An

On cards, draw or paste pictures of desert animals. Categorize them as mammals, birds, reptiles, or insects.

THE DESERT IS THEIRS

Ap

Color, cut out, and paste the desert plants and animals into the scene below.

THE DESERT IS THEIRS

Finish this drawing of the desert.

Name _____

THE DESERT IS THEIRS

WRITING

Ev/Sy **Group Activity:** Pretend that you and your classmates are Desert People. What would you like most about the desert? (Discuss and list ideas on board. Model writing sentences from ideas generated.)

Ev/Sy **Pre-Writers:** Draw what you would like most about the desert if you lived in one. Copy and complete the sentence: "I like the desert because _____ ."

Ev/Sy **Beginning Writers:** Draw and write what you think you would like most about the desert.

Ev/Sy **Experienced Writers:** Write about two or three things you think you would like most about the desert. Illustrate your work when you are done.

LANGUAGE ARTS

K/C **Author! Author!** Read other books by Byrd Baylor to get the feel of the desert. (Some other books by this author are *Everyone Needs A Rock, I'm In Charge Of Celebrations, Hawk, I'm Your Brother, If You Are A Hunter Of Fossils,* and *The Way To Start A Day.*)

Sy **Legends:** Make up your own legends about Coyote, Spider, Hawk, and the other desert animals. Tell how these animals helped the earth.

MATHEMATICS

K/An **Temperature:** Keep track of the temperature in your area and of the temperature in the Southwest by watching TV weather reports. Compare and contrast the temperatures in the two areas. Discuss how your life would change if you lived in the Southwest. (Choose another area of the country to compare with the Southwest if you live in the Southwest.)

SOCIAL STUDIES

K **Desert People:** Study desert Indian tribes: Papago, Hopi, Zuni, Navaho. Learn about their food, dress, homes, and culture.

FINE ARTS

Ap **Sewing Earth And Sky:** Draw or paint separate pictures of the earth and sky. (Use a hole punch to poke holes along one side of each picture. Have the children sew them together with yarn.)

Ap **Weaving:** Weave placemats out of strips of construction paper. Discuss how the Desert People weave blankets and baskets.

IN SHADOWLAND

Summary: Shadowland is the place shadows go in the sunless days of winter. When the watchman of Shadowland helps a poor matchgirl in the real world, both worlds become confused.

PREREADING DISCUSSION:

Have you ever seen your shadow? Where do you think your shadow goes when the sun is gone? (Discuss.)

This is a story about a make-believe place called Shadowland where all shadows go in the dark days of winter. Listen to the differences between Shadowland and the real world.

POSTREADING DISCUSSION:

What are the differences between Shadowland and the real world? (List on board.)

SHADOWLAND   REAL WORLD

K **EXPERIMENT:**
The Sun Makes Day And Night

You will need:
- Student reproducible page 128
- A flashlight
- A globe

1. Shine the flashlight (sun) on the globe. Slowly turn the globe so that it makes complete rotations.

2. Where the sun is shining on the rotating earth, it is day; where it isn't shining, it is night.

3. Color day and night and answer questions on reproducible page.

IN SHADOWLAND

EARTH ORBIT – WHOLE GROUP

K/Ap

Act out the earth's orbit by walking around a student holding a cut-out of the sun. (Explain that the earth orbits the sun once every year.)

ME AND MY SHADOW – INDIVIDUALS, PAIRS, OR COOPERATIVE GROUPS

K/Ap

Record how shadows change during the course of the day. Go outside once every hour and stand on a marked spot. Have someone trace around your shadow on the ground. (Use chalk on blacktop or marking pens on butcher paper. Explain that the change in shadow length is caused by the earth's rotation around the sun.) When the sun is at different locations in the sky, shadows change.

ACT IT OUT – PAIRS, COOPERATIVE GROUPS, OR WHOLE GROUP

Sy

Act out activities you do during the day, and those you do at night. Other students will watch your pantomime and try to guess what the activities are.

WHAT IF . . . – PAIRS OR COOPERATIVE GROUPS

Ev

Discuss what kinds of things might happen if we didn't have day and night. Would plants grow? What would animals eat? Would there be weather? What would the earth look like? ("Chain" students' responses.)

Example:

What if no day or night?	plants wouldn't grow	nothing for animals to eat	animals would die	people would die	no life on Earth

SOLAR ECLIPSE – WHOLE GROUP

K

A solar eclipse happens when the moon moves directly between the sun and the earth and the moon blocks out the sun's light for a period of time. People in ancient times thought a terrible monster was eating the sun and were afraid. Today we know this is just an eclipse.

IN SHADOWLAND

Color day (blue or green) and night (black) in the correct place.

Is it day or night?

Draw and write what you would be doing.

It is _____.

I would be _____

_____.

Is it day or night?

Draw and write what you would be doing.

It is _____.

I would be _____

_____.

Name _____

IN SHADOWLAND

SUNDIAL

You can tell time by the sun.
Cut out the circle.
Paste it on a piece of cardboard.
Put a pencil through the middle.
Place it on the ground in the sun as shown,
    with pencil point in the ground.
Mark where the shadow falls every hour.

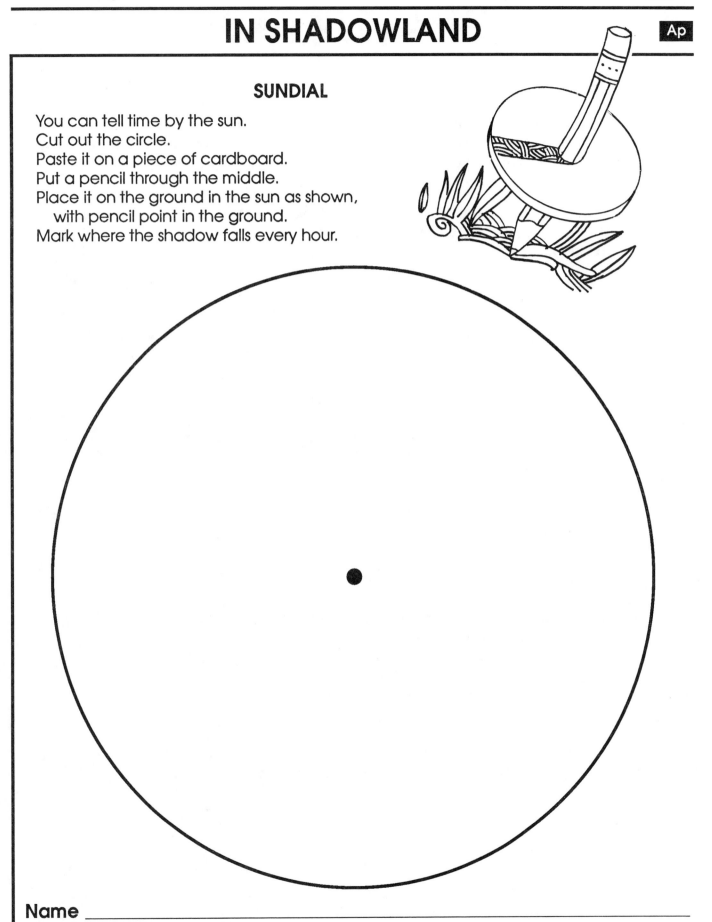

Name _____

IN SHADOWLAND

WRITING

Sy **Group Activity:** Pretend you are a shadow in Shadowland. What kind of shadow would you be? Where would you go in the real world when the sun came out? (Discuss and model writing sentences from student responses. Encourage original ideas in children's writing.)

Sy **Pre-Writers:** Draw the shadow you would want to be, then draw what you look like in the real world. Copy and complete the sentences: "I am a _____ shadow. I live in _____ ."

Sy **Beginning Writers:** Draw and write about yourself in Shadowland and in the real world.

Sy **Experienced Writers:** Write about the kind of shadow you would be in Shadowland and where you would go in the real world when the sun came out. Illustrate your work.

LANGUAGE ARTS

C/Ap **Puppet Show:** Retell the story or make up other Shadowland stories.

Ap **Shadow Puppets:** Make shadow puppets with your hands.

MATHEMATICS

K **Measuring:** Measure the length of your own shadow. Select a few classmates and measure their shadows.

SOCIAL STUDIES

K **Who's Awake / Who's Asleep?** Learn about the countries who have night when we have day, and vice versa.

K **Sundial:** Study the ancient cultures who used sundials before clocks were invented.

FINE ARTS

Ap **Cut Out Shadows:** Draw and cut out scenes on black paper. Paste them onto white paper to create a "Shadowland" character.

GRANDFATHER TWILIGHT

Summary: Grandfather Twilight takes a pearl each evening and walks to the ocean. It grows larger with each step until he gives it to the sea. Then it becomes the luminous moon.

PREREADING DISCUSSION:

Is the moon always in the sky? When does it usually come out? (Discuss.)

This is a make-believe story about how the moon gets in the sky. While you listen to it, think of the things you know about the moon.

POSTREADING DISCUSSION:

What do you know about the moon? Is it always the same shape? (Discuss.)

K CONCEPT:
The Moon

The moon is a satellite that orbits the earth. Unlike the earth, it has no air on it. It takes one month for the moon to orbit the earth. In that time, the moon goes through phases where it looks as if it changes shape.

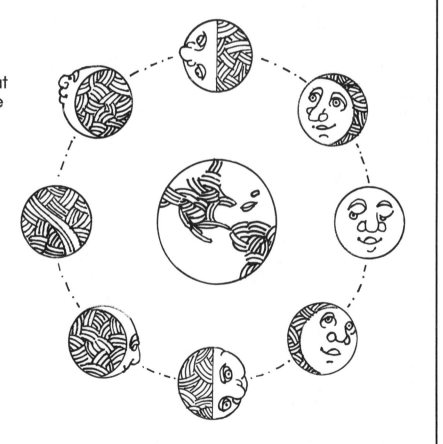

GRANDFATHER TWILIGHT

CHART PHASES – INDIVIDUALS OR WHOLE GROUP

K Keep a record of the moon phases every day for a month. Record the phases on a calendar.

FARMER'S ALMANAC – COOPERATIVE GROUPS OR WHOLE GROUP

K Read and discuss what the almanac has to say about planting and doing other things by the moon.

MOON EXPEDITION – INDIVIDUALS, PAIRS, COOPERATIVE GROUPS, OR WHOLE GROUP

Ap Pretend you are going on an expedition to the moon. Do some research on the lunar landscape. Where will you want to land, and why? Talk about the questions you will want answered, what to pack, and how long you'll be gone. Make lists of things you will need (oxygen, spacesuit, radio, etc.).

MOON ROCK COLLECTOR – INDIVIDUALS, PAIRS, OR COOPERATIVE GROUPS

Ap While on your expedition to the moon, you must collect samples of moon rocks and soil. The teacher will provide boxes, cardboard tubes, wires, and other objects that you will use to create a "moon rock collector." (Have children test their collectors in the sandbox when they're complete.)

LUNAR LANDSCAPE – INDIVIDUALS, PAIRS, OR COOPERATIVE GROUPS

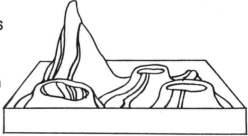

Ap You will need: • Paper plates or shallow boxes
• Plaster of paris
Look at a map of the moon. The teacher will point out craters and mountains. Then fashion your own lunar landscape of plaster of paris in a paper plate or shallow box.

GRANDFATHER TWILIGHT

K/An

THE MOON

Unscramble the letters to make words to fill in the blanks.

| a e i l t s l e t | The moon is a _____ . |

| t o b r i | It takes one month to _____ the earth. |

New moon

New Crescent

1st Quarter

New Gibbous

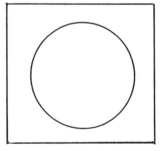
Full moon

Old Gibbous

3rd Quarter

Old Crescent

| s h e a s p | The pictures above show the _____ of the moon. |

Name _____

GRANDFATHER TWILIGHT

WRITING

`An` **Group Activity:** How is the moon like a pearl? How are they different? (List ideas on board. Model writing sentences from student responses.)

`An` **Pre-Writers:** Draw one way the moon is like a pearl and one way it is different. Copy and complete this sentence: "The moon is _____ and _____ ."

`An` **Beginning Writers:** Draw and write about how the moon is like a pearl and how it is different.

`An` **Experienced Writers:** Write two or three ways the moon is similar to and different from a pearl. Illustrate your work.

LANGUAGE ARTS

`Sy` **Trip To The Moon:** Tell or write about an imaginary trip to the moon.

`C` **Lunar Legends:** Read about or make up stories about how the moon got into the sky.

MATHEMATICS

`K` **Fractions:** Study fractions along with phases of the moon (whole, half, quarter).

SOCIAL STUDIES

`K` **Old Sayings:** Interview adults to learn sayings about the moon like "full moon fever" and "howl at the moon."

`K/Ev` **Moon Phases And Feelings:** Discuss and record feelings people might have during a full moon or a new moon.

FINE ARTS

`Ap` **Mobile:** Make mobiles of the sun, earth, and moon out of coat hangers.

`Ap` **Torn Paper Moonscape:** Construct torn-paper pictures of a moonscape.

REGARDS TO THE MAN IN THE MOON

Summary: Louie's father isn't just the junkman the kids tease Louie about. He encourages Louie to use his imagination to build a rocket ship for a trip into outer space.

PREREADING DISCUSSION:

What do you imagine you might see in outer space? (Discuss)

This is a story of Louie and his imaginary trip into space. Listen to what he sees.

POSTREADING DISCUSSION:

What did Louie see in outer space? What other planets and things do you think he might see? (List on board.)

 ACTIVITY:
The Solar System

You will need:
- Student reproducible page 137
- 12 x 18 black construction paper for each child
- Scissors
- Glue

Our solar system consists of one star, nine planets, and an asteroid belt.

Look at the reproducible page. Write down in the blanks provided the number of moons owned by each planet and a number showing the place of each planet in the Solar System.

Cut out the planets and paste them on the black paper in the right places. Draw in the asteroid belt between Mars and Jupiter.

REGARDS TO THE MAN IN THE MOON

OPERATION PLANET – INDIVIDUALS, PAIRS, COOPERATIVE GROUPS, OR WHOLE GROUP

`K/Ev`

Research the different planets and then do the following for each one:
1. Draw an accurate picture of the planet and its moons (if any).
2. Write a description of it.
3. List five important facts about the planet.
4. Make a diorama or model of its surface.
5. Describe a day on its surface (length of day as well as weather).

SPACE CENTER – INDIVIDUALS, PAIRS, OR COOPERATIVE GROUPS

`Ap/Sy`

The class will paint a mural backdrop of space on butcher paper or an old sheet, then construct a spaceship out of boxes (a refrigerator box is great). Take your own imaginary space trip, then tape record or write about it in a "Space Log" kept at the center.

CLASS MOBILE – COOPERATIVE GROUPS OR WHOLE GROUP

`Ap`

Construct papier mâché models of each of the planets. Paint them and hang them from the ceiling of the classroom with a brief description of each.

SATURN

WHERE ARE YOU IN THE SOLAR SYSTEM – WHOLE GROUP

`Ap`

On the playground, members of the class will arrange themselves as the sun, the planets, and the earth's moon. (Draw each one's orbit around the sun. All should start in a straight line and walk at the same rate.) Observe how some planets orbit faster than others.

JET PROPULSION EXPERIMENT – PAIRS, COOPERATIVE GROUPS, OR WHOLE GROUP

`K/Ap`

You will need: • Wire or fishing line
                 • Drinking straws
                 • Tape
                 • Balloons

This illustrates how rocket action works.
1. Tape the drinking straw to the balloon and thread the wire through the straw. Fasten ends of the wire to chairs or other convenient holders.
2. Blow up the balloon and let it go.
3. Measure the distance it travels.
4. Set up experiment so balloon will travel vertically. Measure distance.

REGARDS TO THE MAN IN THE MOON   K

THE SOLAR SYSTEM

For each planet, fill in the blanks to show number of moons and order in Solar System.

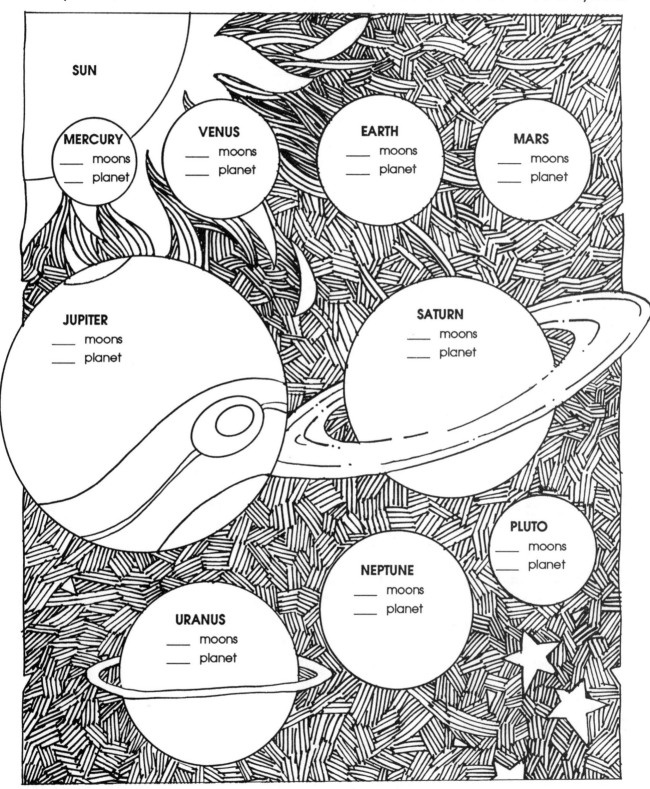

SUN

MERCURY
___ moons
___ planet

VENUS
___ moons
___ planet

EARTH
___ moons
___ planet

MARS
___ moons
___ planet

JUPITER
___ moons
___ planet

SATURN
___ moons
___ planet

PLUTO
___ moons
___ planet

NEPTUNE
___ moons
___ planet

URANUS
___ moons
___ planet

Name _____

REGARDS TO THE MAN IN THE MOON

WRITING

Ap **Group Activity:** Write a chart story about what you would see if you went into space.

Ap **Pre-Writers:** Draw what you would see if you went into space. Copy and complete this sentence: "I would see _____ in space."

Ap **Beginning Writers:** Draw and write what you would see if you went into space.

Ap **Experienced Writers:** Write about two or three things you would see in space. Illustrate them.

LANGUAGE ARTS

Ap **Tin Can Communication:** Communicate using tin can telephones. Tell everything about the blast-off and space mission.

Ap/Sy **Space Log:** Write a log of an imaginary space flight.

MATHEMATICS

K/Ap **Planetary Calendar Conversions:** Figure out the time in days and years it takes planets to orbit the sun. Convert into months and days.

Ap **Comparative Measuring:** The class will gather in the schoolyard. (Determine comparative distances between the planets and stand a student at each interval.)

SOCIAL STUDIES

K **Galileo And The Telescope:** Discuss how people learned about the solar system before space flight was possible. (Galileo was the inventor of the telescope. Many of his discoveries were censored by the church.)

K **How The Planets Got Their Names:** Ancient Roman gods were the source of the names for the planets. Learn about the gods and the myths of their powers.

FINE ARTS

Ap **Mobile:** Make mobiles of the sun, earth, and moon out of coat hangers.

Ap **Junk Sculpture:** Make space sculptures out of things on a junk table.

Ap **Space Helmet:** Construct a helmet for space flight out of boxes, aluminum foil, wire, and other spaceworthy material.

THE LEGEND OF THE MILKY WAY

Summary: An earthly man and a heavenly princess marry. When the Queen of Heaven finds out about the marriage, she calls the princess back to the sky and blocks her husband's following with a river of stars.

PREREADING DISCUSSION:

Have you seen the stars in the sky? How do you think they got there? (Discuss.)

This is a make-believe story told by the Chinese people about the stars. Listen for what happened first, second, and third. While you listen, think of the stars you've seen.

POSTREADING DISCUSSION:

An

What happened first, second, and third in the story? (List on board.)

K **CONCEPT:**
Constellations

You will need:

- Student reproducible page 141
- Black paint
- Straight pins (1 for each child)
- Blue crayons
- Toilet paper tube (1 for each child)

1. Paint a toilet paper tube black inside and out. This is your telescope.

2. Color blue and cut out the constellation circles on reproducible page.

3. With a straight pin poke holes through constellation stars.

4. Look at the "constellations" through the "telescopes" and identify them.

THE LEGEND OF THE MILKY WAY

WHAT MAKES UP A GALAXY? – COOPERATIVE GROUPS OR WHOLE GROUP

K

A galaxy is a system of stars grouped together into a revolving mass. Our galaxy is called the Milky Way because on clear nights parts of the sky looks milky. The milky color is actually the light from millions of faraway stars in our galaxy.

Discuss the many types of things that exist in our galaxy: binary stars, comets, nebulae, black holes, pulsars, etc. Each student can prepare a short report on one of these phenomena by showing pictures or a diorama and explaining it as if he or she were an astronaut.

BIG BANG MURAL – INDIVIDUALS, PAIRS, OR COOPERATIVE GROUPS

Ap

Scientists believe all the galaxies and things in the universe were brought into being by a gigantic explosion called the "BIG BANG." Have the class illustrate the Big Bang and all it created by drawing a mural of it.

LIFE OF A STAR – COOPERATIVE GROUPS OR WHOLE GROUP

K/C

Learn about different kinds of stars and the life cycle of a star.

Our sun is a star.

Red Giant

White Dwarf

Nova

TELESCOPES – COOPERATIVE GROUPS OR WHOLE GROUP

K

The teacher will describe how a basic refraction telescope works. (On a clear night — Open House or Back-to-School Night are good — meet with the class and look at various stars through telescopes.)

WHY STARS MOVE – WHOLE GROUP

K

You will need: • Dark umbrella • Globe • Tape • Pipe cleaners
The reason the stars appear to move is that the earth rotates.

1. The teacher will put paper stars in constellations on the underside of the umbrella.
2. The teacher will fashion a pipe cleaner stick figure and tape it to your location on the globe.
3. The teacher will open the umbrella over the globe and begin rotating the globe. The children will move with the pipe cleaner figure as the globe turns. Notice how the stars seem to move.

CLASS PLANETARIUM – INDIVIDUALS, PAIRS, COOPERATIVE GROUPS, OR WHOLE GROUP

Ap

You will need: • Toilet tube telescopes and constellations • Flashlights
After completing the constellation activity, darken the classroom and shine flashlights through the cardboard tubes to project the constellations onto the ceiling. (Once the basic 6 have been identified, introduce other constellations.)

THE LEGEND OF THE MILKY WAY

CONSTELLATIONS

Color constellations blue and cut them out.

Poke pin through stars on each constellation.

Look at them through your telescope.

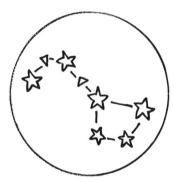

Ursa Major
(Big Dipper)

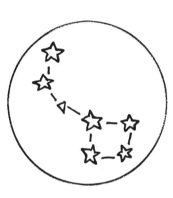

Ursa Minor
(Little Dipper)

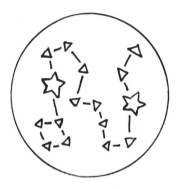

Draco
(The Dragon)

Cassiopeia

Cepheus

Orion

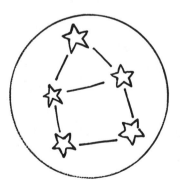

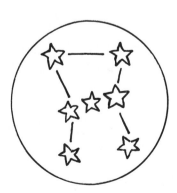

Name _____

THE LEGEND OF THE MILKY WAY

WRITING

Ap/Sy   **Group Activity:** Discuss information listed on the board from postreading activity. (Model writing sentences or a paragraph from it.)

Ap/Sy   **Pre-Writers:** Draw the first, second, and third thing that happened in the story. Number them.

Ap/Sy   **Beginning Writers:** Draw and write the three main things that happened in the story.

Ap/Sy   **Experienced Writers:** Write your own paragraph about the main events of the story. Illustrate your work.

LANGUAGE ARTS

Sy   **New Legends:** Tell or write your own legends about how the Milky Way or constellations got their names.

K/C   **Greek Mythology:** Listen to stories from Greek mythology about how constellations got their names.

MATHEMATICS

K   **Constellation Addition:** Count stars in various constellations — add, subtract, and multiply them.

K/Ap   **Galactic Numbers:** Make a bulletin board of an imaginary galaxy. Students add stars to it to equal a large, predetermined number: 1,000 or 10,000.

SOCIAL STUDIES

K   **Star Navigators:** Learn about the way people navigate by the stars using the North Star as a guide.

K/C   **Star Map:** Map the brightest stars in the sky on a given night. Find out the names of all the constellations the next day in class.

FINE ARTS

Ap   **Poke A Constellation:** Take a straight pin and poke constellations into black construction paper.

Ap   **Pantomime:** Act out legends of how constellations got their names.

BIBLIOGRAPHY

MEASUREMENT

- Length – *Inch By Inch,* by Leo Lionni. NY: Astor-Honor, Inc., 1960.
- Large Number Concepts – *How Much Is A Million?* by David Schwartz. NY: Scholastic, 1985.

NUTRITION

- Food Groups – *Gregory, The Terrible Eater,* by Mitchell Sharmat. NY: Scholastic, 1980.
- Junk Food – *Bread And Jam For Frances,* by Russell Hoban. NY: Harper & Row, 1964.
- Healthy Snacks – *Munching, Poems About Eating,* by Lee Bennett Hopkins. Boston: Little, Brown and Co., 1985.

SEASONS

- Attributes Of Seasons – *Summer Is . . . ,* by Charlotte Zolotow. NY: Thomas Y. Crowell, 1967.
- Dressing Appropriately – *Thomas' Snowsuit,* by Robert Munsch. Toronto: Annick Press Ltd., 1985.

WEATHER

- Rain Cycle – *Bringing The Rain To Kapiti Plain,* by Verna Aardema. NY: Dial Books, 1981.
- Wind – *Housekeeper Of The Wind,* by Christine Widman. NY: Harper & Row, 1990.
- Clouds – *The Cloud Book,* by Tomie dePaola. NY: Holiday House, 1975.
- Rainbows – *The Rainbow Rider,* by Jane Yolen. NY: Thomas Y. Crowell, 1974.

PLANTS

- Seeds / Plant Cycle – *The Tiny Seed,* by Eric Carle. MA: Picture Book Studio, 1987.
- What Plants Need – *The Plant Sitter,* by Gene Zion. NY: Scholastic, 1969.
- Trees Are Necessary– *A Tree Is Nice,* by Janice Udry. NY: Harper & Row, 1956.

ANIMALS

- Pets – *A Pet For Mrs. Arbuckle,* by Gwenda Smyth. NY: Crown Publishers, 1981.
- Farm Animals – *The Day Jimmy's Boa Ate The Wash,* by Trinka Noble. NY: Dial Books, 1980.
- Fish /Amphibians – *Fish Is Fish,* by Leo Lionni. NY: Alfred A. Knopf, 1970.
- Mammals – *Animals Born Alive And Well,* by Ruth Heller. NY: Grosset & Dunlap, 1982.
- Animal Coverings – *Animals Should Definitely Not Wear Clothing,* by Judi Barrett. Hartford: Connecticut Printers, 1970.
- Animals From Eggs – *Chickens Aren't The Only Ones,* by Ruth Heller. NY: Grosset & Dunlap, 1981.

HABITATS

- Who Lives In A Garden – *The Snail's Spell,* by Joanne Ryder. NY: Puffin Books, 1982.
- Desert – *The Desert Is Theirs,* by Byrd Baylor. NY: Aladdin Books, 1975.
- Rainforest – *Rain Forest,* by Helen Cowcher. NY: Farrar, Straus & Giroux, 1990.
- Animal Camouflage /Adaptation – *How To Hide A Polar Bear,* by Ruth Heller. NY: Grosset & Dunlap, 1985.
- Meadow/ Woodlands – *Under The Moon,* by Joanne Ryder. NY: Just Right Books, 1989.

ASTRONOMY

- Sun – *In Shadowland,* by Mitsumasa Anno. NY: Orchard Books, 1988.
- Moon – *Grandfather Twilight,* by Barbara Berger. NY: Philomel Books, 1984.
- Solar System – *Regards To The Man In The Moon,* by Ezra Jack Keats. NY: Aladdin Books, 1981.
- Constellations – *The Legend Of The Milky Way,* by Jeanne M. Lee. NY: Henry Holt, 1982.

888